Foreword

This report examines Denmark's foreign direct investment policies. It is the result of an examination held in June 1994 by an OECD Working Group made up of representatives of the Committee on Capital Movements and Invisible Transactions (CMIT) and the Committee on International Investment and Multinational Enterprises (CIME). These committees, whose members are officials from ministries of finance, foreign affairs, commerce and industry, and from central banks, promote liberal, non-discriminatory investment policies through the OECD Code of Liberalisation of Capital Movements and the National Treatment Instrument.

Following the Working Group examination, this report was reviewed and adopted by the CMIT and CIME. Factual updating has been made through October 1994. The report was approved and derestricted by the OECD Council on 22 February 1995.

Table of contents

Chapter 1

Introduction and summary

As in other OECD countries, Denmark's FDI inflows and outflows grew in the late 1980s. Foreign direct investment into Denmark has been rather low when compared to other OECD countries of comparable size, however, both in the aggregate and in relation to GDP. The Danish authorities would welcome more FDI into the country, particularly for the technology and competition they hope it would bring to the Danish economy, but they are not contemplating any special incentives for foreign investors.

Denmark's FDI laws and policies are generally characterised by openness and non-discrimination. There are no general screening provisions for inward direct investment, the activities where foreign direct investment is restricted are limited, and foreign investors are treated like national firms in most areas of economic activity. Denmark's investment restrictions based on public order and national security, which are limited to the manufacture of war equipment, have been further narrowed by a 1990 law which allows limited foreign participation in firms manufacturing war equipment.

Still, in a number of sectors or activities, investors from outside the EC may be treated differently than those from inside the EC. There are reciprocity provisions for non-EC investors in banking and financial services and insurance, for example. Liberalisation which has taken place in the air transport, and commercial fishing sectors – motivated largely by EC directives – has not been extended to all OECD countries. Moreover, reciprocity may be applied to non-EC investors in activities being liberalised under EC Directives on electricity and natural gas, or according to the EC Directive on rights for oil and gas exploration and development.

A number of other market access issues that affect foreign direct investment are being addressed by the Danish government, largely through the sale of shares in state enterprises, demonopolisation and improving competition law and practice.

While Denmark's public sector is one of the largest in the OECD,[1] the state's direct involvement in the commercial sector has been rather small. The Danish authorities recognise, however, that there are still a number of areas where market access has been limited and where further liberalisation could lead to greater efficiency. Privatisations have already taken place in insurance, the Copenhagen airport, the postal bank, a data processing company and the state telecommunications company. In the most important single privatisation, that of Tele Danmark, the Danish Government is keeping 51 per cent of the company's shares, with the remaining 49 per cent sold in Europe, the United States and locally. Tele Danmark's privatisation may be important as an example for other telecommunications privatisations which have been announced by smaller European countries.

On demonopolisation, the government is also making progress, motivated in part by EC rules on liberalisation of the internal market. The impact of these liberalisations on non-EC investors remains uncertain, however, as reciprocity may be applied to non-EC applicants wishing to participate in newly-liberalised, EC-regulated activities such as electricity and natural gas, and oil and gas exploration and production.

The Danish Government has already repealed DANGAS' sole right to import natural gas, and under an EC proposed Council directive it would appear that DANGAS may also have to surrender its exclusive rights to sell, transport and store natural gas as well. Indeed this decision has already been taken in principle, and would be implemented in the context of EC negotiations on the single market for natural gas. In the event DANGAS' exclusive rights are surrendered, it is envisaged that non-discriminatory rules would apply, and that Danish and non-Danish investors would be treated equally. Authorisation for exploration and development of hydrocarbons may also be liberalised, according to a proposed EC Directive. In telecommunications the Danish Government intends to liberalise the resale of leased line capacity for voice telephone services. Some postal services are also likely to be opened to more private participation.

Competition law and practice is being reviewed and strengthened in Denmark, as a number of important activities remain shielded from competition or are relatively unexposed to market pressures. In the professional services, transportation, construction and distribution sectors, anti-competitive agreements may in some cases still exist, taking the form of price lists, price-setting rules and discount allowances. Increasing competition in the Danish market is an important economic policy objective, and the government is currently working to remove entry regulations that have stifled competition in construction, transportation and trade. A new Competition Act was enacted in 1990 which strengthened the legal framework governing competition among businesses, and gave the competition authorities wide-ranging powers to obtain and disclose information about restrictive business powers. The Danish Competition Council is working to prohibit horizontal agreements on prices and market sharing, and its actions have been confirmed in appeals before the Competition Appeals Tribunal.

The Danish government is also addressing structural and institutional factors that are important to private sector growth, including direct investment growth, and in 1993 announced an industrial policy for that purpose. Direct subsidies to firms will remain low, but more emphasis will go to support for a number of "strongholds" that have been identified as potentially important to industrial competitiveness, as well as support for large established firms and new start-up firms. Foreign direct investment is one part of the industrial policy, where it is hoped that more foreign investment will flow into stronghold areas such as telecommunications, food processing and bio-technology.

Chapter 2

The role of foreign direct investment in Denmark's economy

A. Data, methodological and definitional issues

In Denmark, data on direct investment flows is collected by Danmarks Nationalbank as part of the statistics on payments between Denmark and foreign countries used for the compilation of balance of payments data. Data is published on a quarterly basis by the Bank in a special direct investment report and in the quarterly *Monetary Review* and the Bank's Annual Report.[2] The basis for the Nationalbank's statistics is the 1988 Executive Order on Foreign Exchange Regulations.[3]

Direct investment is defined as an investment conducted with a view to establishing a lasting (*i.e.* the intention of not less than five years) financial relationship between the investor and the enterprise concerned. The investor must also through the investment obtain, maintain or expand access to the exertion of significant influence on the management of the enterprise. In practice, a share of ownership of over 10 per cent is normally regarded as a direct investment.

Direct investment may take the form of the contribution or acquisition of equity capital in a commercial enterprise, or the contribution of funds to a branch. However the stationing of agents or the establishment of representative offices which typically conduct preparatory, auxiliary or contract-furthering activities for the company at home are not registered as direct investment nor are international activities such as licensing, franchising, management contracts and similar undertakings likely to include the transfer of equity capital.

Until 1992, the definition used on direct investment deviated from the OECD/IMF Benchmark definition[4] as inter-company loans and reinvested earnings were not included in the published figures. As from 1992 inter-company loans and acquisition of real property for non-commercial purposes are included in the flow figures. The current account figures include an estimate of reinvested earnings but they lack the necessary details to be included in the foreign invest-ment figures. The lack of information on inter-company loans up to and including 1991 may to some extent explain the relatively low level of foreign direct investment.

A survey on direct investment stock figures has recently been completed.[5] The stock figures are compiled in accordance with the Benchmark definition, including information on reinvested earnings.

Denmarks Nationalbank also published data on the industry breakdown of FDI flows. However, the classification is by industry of affiliates, *i.e.* the com-pany in which the investment is made and not the industry of the investor. This needs to be taken into account in assessing the data.

B. FDI inflows, home countries and sectors

Denmark is a small economy of 5 million people dominated by small and medium sized enterprises operating in traditional industries. Its dependence on the outside world has remained, however, below the levels normally observed in economies of its size and this is particularly apparent with respect to Denmark's exposure to international direct investment which, until a recent past, has been one of lowest among OECD countries (see Annex 4, Table 2).[6]

FDI into Denmark nevertheless took off in the second half of the 1980s after several years of flat growth (Table 1, Chart 1). This took place even though the economy was undergoing a period of macro-economic adjustment and slow growth. Average annual inflows experienced a tenfold increase between 1981-1987 and 1988-1993, adding some US$7 billion to the foreign equity stock in Denmark in the latter period. The stock of FDI has recently been estimated around US$14.7 billion at the end of 1991. The data shows, however, sharp fluctuations because of the influence of single large transactions on any given year.

This favourable trend also shows itself in the FDI contribution to GDP and Gross Fixed Capital Formation (GFCF). While FDI inflows barely exceeded the

Table 1. **Direct investment flows, 1975-1993** [1]

US$ million

	Inward	Outward
1975	267	79
1976	−190	64
1977	76	161
1978	89	33
1979	103	–
1980	106	197
1981	100	141
1982	136	77
1983	64	159
1984	9	93
1985	109	303
1986	161	646
1987	88	618
1988	504	719
1989	1 084	2 027
1990	1 133	1 509
1991	1 530	1 851
1992	1 015	2 225
1993	1 669	1 261

1. Balance of payments statistics.
Source: Danmarks Nationalbank.

Chart 1. **Foreign direct investment flows to and from Denmark, 1975-1993**

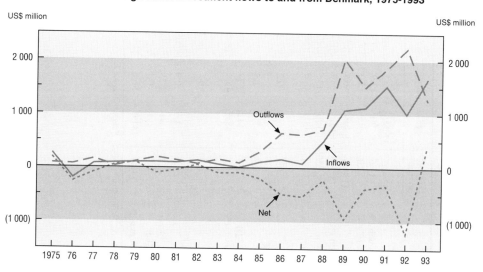

Source: OECD/DAF – Balance of payments data.

13

Table 2. Indicators of international direct investment

US$ million

	1975-1980 average	1981	1982	1983	1984	1985	1986	1987	1988	1989	1990	1991	1992	1993
GDP	52 407	57 246	55 742	56 046	54 582	58 045	82 375	102 321	108 751	104 956	129 753	130 277	142 438	135 273
Nominal growth (%)	11.6	9.1	13.9	10.4	10.3	8.8	8.4	5.0	4.6	4.8	4.7	3.8	3.0	1.8
Real growth (%)	2.0	–0.9	3.0	2.5	4.4	4.3	3.6	0.3	1.2	0.6	2.0	1.2	1.0	0.2
GFCF	11 040	8 959	8 955	8 972	9 390	10 871	17 102	20 179	19 643	19 008	22 983	21 976	21 721	20 030
GFCF growth (%)	..	–18.8	–0.0	0.2	4.7	15.8	57.3	18.0	–2.7	–3.2	20.9	–4.4	–1.2	–7.8
Inflows of FDI	75	100	136	64	9	109	161	88	504	1 084	1 133	1 530	1 015	1 669
Inflow growth (%)	..	33.0	36.0	–52.9	–85.9	1 111.1	47.7	–45.3	472.7	115.1	4.5	35.0	–33.7	64.4
Inflows as % of GDP	0.1	0.2	0.2	0.1	0.0	0.2	0.2	0.1	0.5	1.0	0.9	1.2	0.7	1.2
Inflows as % of GFCF	0.7	1.1	1.5	0.7	0.1	1.0	0.9	0.4	2.6	5.7	4.9	7.0	4.7	8.3
Outflows of FDI	89	141	77	159	93	303	646	618	719	2 027	1 509	1 851	2 225	1 261
Outflow growth (%)	..	58.4	–45.4	106.5	–41.5	225.8	113.2	–4.3	16.3	181.9	–25.6	22.7	20.2	–43.3
Outflows as a % of GDP	0.2	0.2	0.1	0.3	0.2	0.5	0.8	0.6	0.7	1.9	1.2	1.4	1.6	0.9
Outflows as a % of GFCF	0.8	1.6	0.9	1.8	1.0	2.8	3.8	3.1	3.7	10.7	6.6	8.4	10.2	6.3
Inflows – Outflows	–14	–41	59	–95	–84	–194	–485	–530	–215	–943	–376	–321	–1 210	408
as a % of GDP	0.0	–0.1	0.1	–0.2	–0.2	–0.3	–0.6	–0.5	–0.2	–0.9	–0.3	–0.2	–0.8	0.3
Outflows/Inflows (%)	118.4	141.0	56.6	248.4	1 033.3	278.0	401.2	702.3	142.7	187.0	133.2	121.0	219.2	75.6

Source: Danmarks Nationalbank; OECD *National Accounts of OECD Countries*; *OECD Economic Outlook*.

levels of 0.1-0.2 per cent of GDP and 1 per cent of GFCF during 1981-1987, they accounted for over 1 per cent of GDP and 5 per cent of GFCF between 1988 and 1993. These percentages reached a peak of 1.2 and 8.3 respectively in 1993 (Table 2, Chart 2). A significant portion of these investments were in the form of mergers and acquisitions as opposed to greenfield investments, which was facilitated by the small average size of Danish firms (see Annex 3, Table 1).

Europe has provided the bulk of FDI into Denmark and this became even more pronounced after the adoption of the Single Market programme when Nordic countries, and more particularly Sweden, started to use Denmark as a more active platform for their operations in the EEC. While EEC countries represented 43 per cent of inward direct investment since 1988, Nordic countries accounted for 40 per cent of the total and Sweden alone for 22 per cent (Table 3, Chart 3).

Germany (11 per cent), Netherlands (10 per cent), the United Kingdom (8 per cent) were the other major single source countries. Forty per cent of FDI inflows were recorded as originating from Belgium-Luxembourg but to a large

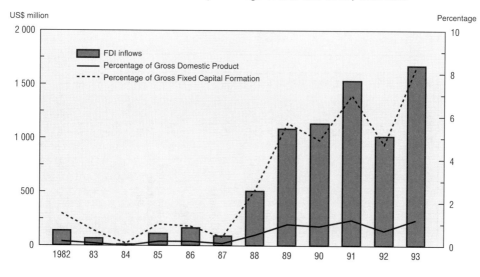

Chart 2. **FDI inflows as a percentage of GDP and GFCF, 1982-1993**

US$ million

Percentage

FDI inflows
Percentage of Gross Domestic Product
Percentage of Gross Fixed Capital Formation

Source: OECD/DAF.

15

Table 3. Foreign direct investment flows into Denmark by country, 1982-1993

DKr million

	1982-1987 average	% of total	1988-1993 average	% of total	1988	1989	1990	1991	1992	1993
OECD AREA	851	93.1	7 424	98.9	4 002	7 704	7 377	9 249	6 213	9 996
Europe	1 038	113.5	6 670	88.8	2 601	7 231	6 956	8 835	4 938	9 459
EEC	-87	-9.5	3 237	43.1	645	3 034	3 062	4 297	4 490	3 896
Belgium-Luxembourg	-10	-1.1	214	2.9	17	7	163	1 265	613	-780
France	-31	-3.4	835	11.1	117	2 875	293	1 382	16	325
Germany	132	14.4	962	12.8	247	106	548	479	2 266	2 127
Ireland	1	0.1	-155	-2.1		10	2		179	-1 121
Italy	-40	-4.3	39	0.5	-8	6	4	11	181	37
Netherlands	-5	-0.6	744	9.9	279	464	845	827	817	1 233
United Kingdom	-77	-8.4	607	8.1	58	-395	1 205	339	411	2 025
Other Europe	1 125	123.1	3 433	45.7	1 956	4 197	3 894	4 538	448	5 563
Nordic countries[1]	1 243	136.0	2 969	39.5	1 880	4 146	3 569	4 213	186	3 822
Switzerland	-120	-13.1	447	6.0	75	56	311	310	243	1 686
North America	-201	-22.0	658	8.8	1 287	272	344	338	1 206	498
Canada	-14	-1.5	1	0.0	-6	4	-4	-2	30	-18
USA	-187	-20.5	657	8.7	1 293	268	348	340	1 176	516
Other OECD countries	14	1.6	96	1.3	114	201	77	76	69	39
Japan	17	1.9	76	1.0	98	198	32	76	38	15
NON OECD AREA	63	6.9	86	1.1	-611	217	88	84	-86	823
Africa	-5	-0.6	-11	-0.1	1	-97		3	23	3
Central and Eastern Europe	1	0.1	22	0.3	8	29	5	9	12	66
Latin America-Carribean	51	5.5	-11	-0.1	-634	337	51	71	-477	588
South and East Asia	13	1.5	69	0.9	7	-48	17		395	42
DAEs[2]	5	0.5	41	0.5	7	-50	17		234	35
Other Asia	9	0.9	28	0.4		2			161	7
Other countries[3]	-4	-0.5	13	0.2	-6	-8	12	-1	-41	123
TOTAL	914	100.0	7 509	100.0	3 391	7 921	7 465	9 333	6 127	10 819

1. Including Scandinavian Airline System's investments in Denmark.
2. Including Philippines.
3. Including the European countries Gibraltar, Andorra, Malta and Cyprus.
Source: Danmarks Nationalbank.

Chart 3. **Foreign direct investment flows to Denmark**

Breakdown by country

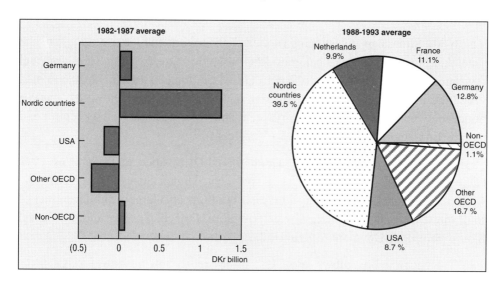

Breakdown by industry

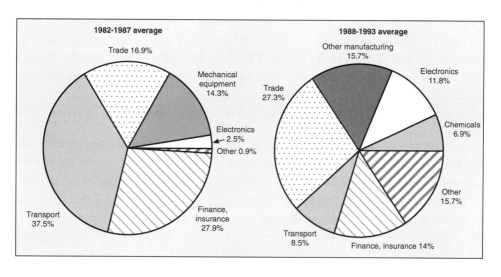

Source: OECD/DAF.

17

extent, they were the investments of foreign multinational enterprises based in this country. Switzerland (6 per cent) started to reinvest again after a retreat during in the first half of the decade. German and Dutch investments have become particularly strong since 1990.

North American investments (notably US investments) were modest in the second half of the 1980's (9 per cent), their relative share dropping from the level registered in the early 1980's (40 per cent of the total in 1982). Japan invested very little in both periods. Latin America and South East Asia, however, made a noticeable contribution in 1992 (6 per cent and 4 per cent) as well as central and eastern European countries in 1993 (5 per cent).

This pattern is confirmed by Denmark's FDI position at the end of 1991 (EC, 45 per cent, Nordic countries 37 per cent, United States, 12 per cent and Japan 0.6 per cent) . The country FDI distribution is also largely similar to that of trade since Germany, Sweden, United Kingdom, France, Norway and the United States were both Denmark's main trading partners (Annex 3, Table 2).

The sectoral breakdown provides further indication on how foreign firms have exploited Denmark's as well as their own comparative advantages. From 1982 to 1987, secondary industry attracted 30 per cent of total FDI and tertiary, 86 per cent while the primary sector experienced a net decline, in part as a result of divestment in the oil sector. The corresponding distribution for 1988-1993 was 34 per cent for the secondary sector, 60 per cent for the tertiary sector and 5.5 per cent for the primary sector (Table 4, Chart 4). The prominence of services is a reflection of the relative importance of this area of activity in the Danish economy, which is also above OECD average. The relative strength of manufacturing is an indicator of the adaptability and productivity of the Danish economy.

Evidence of this is found in the electric and electronic equipment and chemical products which became the main recipients of FDI in the secondary sector (12 per cent and 7 per cent of total FDI in 1987-1993) while in the fist half of the 1980's the sums attracted were much more modest. At the same time, the share of mechanical equipment dropped from 14.3 per cent to 4.2 of FDI inflows between the two periods. In tertiary, the most spectacular gains were in wholesale and retail trade (27 per cent of the total) which eroded somewhat the leading position of finance, insurance and business services (14 per cent instead of 28 per cent) and transport and storage (8 per cent against 32 per cent previously).[7]

Table 4. **Foreign direct investment flows to Denmark by industry, 1982-1993**[1]

DKr million

	1982-1987 average	% of total	1988-1993 average	% of total	1988	1989	1990	1991	1992	1993
PRIMARY	-147	-16.1	416	5.5	336	316	321	77	376	1 069
SECONDARY	277	30.3	2 586	34.4	1 066	1 239	3 375	3 725	3 204	2 907
Food, beverages and tobacco	-53	-5.8	107	1.4	102	121	839	210	154	-785
Textiles, leather and clothing	-7	-0.7	-3	-0.0	-1	93	-138	30	..	..
Paper, printing and publishing	15	1.7	-10	-0.1	117	25	41	-245	..	1 607
Chemical products	49	5.4	520	6.9	130	255	510	320	300	
Coal and petroleum products	19	2.0	-29	-0.4	151	-340	8	8	..	..
Non-metallic products	29	3.1	239	3.2	204	130	1 059	41	..	..
Metal products	29	3.2	74	1.0	41	98	174	131	..	784
Mechanical equipment	130	14.3	319	4.2	18	116	365	68	560	
Electric and electronic equipment	23	2.5	887	11.8	287	669	436	3 062	674	195
Other transport equipment	27	2.9	26	0.3	10	64	79	–	..	1 106
Other manufacturing	16	1.8	457	6.1	7	8	2	100	1 516	
TERTIARY	785	85.8	4 470	59.5	1 989	6 366	3 769	5 407	2 447	6 843
Construction	13	1.4	257	3.4	21	418	457	646	..	2 945
Wholesale and retail trade	155	16.9	2 052	27.3	-300	1 761	1 363	3 891	2 653	87
Transport and storage	343	37.5	640	8.5	746	2 138	762	247	-142	
Finance, insurance and business services	255	27.9	1 052	14.0	1 523	1 998	459	602	-158	1 885
Other services	19	2.1	470	6.3	-1	51	728	21	94	1 926
UNALLOCATED	..	..	37	0.5	..	..	..	124	100	..
TOTAL	914	100.0	7 509	100.0	3 391	7 921	7 465	9 333	6 127	10 819

1. The distribution by sector concerns the company in which investment is made. In certain cases the distribution by sector is estimated for the period 1983 to 1988.
Source: Danmarks Nationalbank.

Chart 4. **Direct investment flows abroad**

Breakdown by country

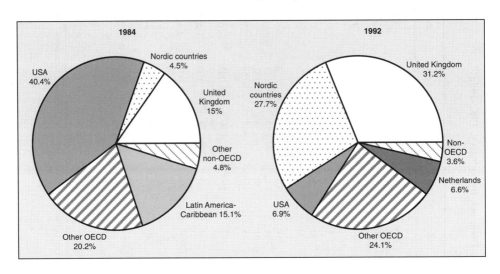

Breakdown by industry

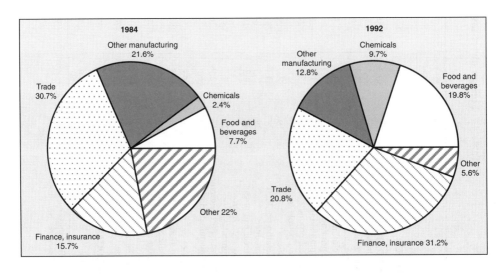

Source: OECD/DAF.

Geography, economic complementarities and the performance of Danish economic agents have therefore been strong inducements for increased foreign investment in Denmark in recent years. The efforts recently deployed by the Danish government to improve the business environment and the growth prospects of the economy[8] suggest that the trend could be sustained in the foreseeable future. It remains to be seen how the entry of Finland, Norway and Sweden into the European Union will affect their investment patterns since the mid-1980's. The Danish authorities are confident that Denmark could become an even more attractive place to invest particularly as the integration between Scandinavia, the new markets around the Baltic sea and other European countries continue develop toward their full potential.

C. FDI outflows, host countries and sectors

Except for 1993, Denmark outgoing direct investment has exceeded ingoing direct investment since the early 1980's. The gap widened significantly when FDI outflows started to rise sharply in 1985, three years before the upturn recorded on the inflows side. Outward flows averaged US$1.2 billion between 1985-1993 against US$100 million between 1975-1984 and the imbalance between inflows and outflows grew from US$105 million to US$520 million between the two periods. Since the mid-1980's, outward direct investment has averaged one per cent of GDP. The percentage for 1992 (1.6 per cent) was one of the highest in the OECD area. The accumulated outward stock at the end of 1991 (91 billion Danish Kroners – DKr) had, as a result, slightly surpassed the accumulated inward stock (87 billion DKr) (Annex 3, Table 3). While this can be attributed to geographical and sectoral considerations to be described below, it has also been a consequence of Denmark's high saving ratio which has provided a capital surplus for investment abroad.

The patterns for country and sectoral destination is quite similar to that already noted for inward direct investment and trade relations which suggests the existence of significant synergies and a fair degree of stability in Denmark's external economic relations. Europe generally (78 per cent in 1985-1992) and the EC in particular (61 per cent in 1985-1992) were the main recipients of Denmark's FDI and the EC pull became even stronger in the second half the 80's (in 1984, the EC share was only 31 per cent) (Table 5). This is also reflected in

Table 5. Direct investment flows abroad by country, 1982-1993

DKr million

	1982	1983	1984	% of total	1985	1986	1987	1988	1989	1990	1991	1992	85-92 average	% of total	1993
OECD AREA	541	772	1 976	80.2	2 498	5 014	3 589	5 099	15 110	9 661	12 043	13 013	8 253	94.2	7 276
Europe	287	–84	899	36.5	1 703	2 946	2 852	3 508	14 144	8 457	9 409	11 743	6 845	78.1	4 182
EEC	124	290	765	31.0	1 369	2 124	2 406	3 046	12 469	6 752	6 504	7 960	5 329	60.8	–1 205
Belgium-Luxembourg	–58	11	–39	–1.6	66	164	64	311	76	105	509	891	273	3.1	–1 456
France	124	130	196	8.0	84	221	159	130	2 483	2 872	461	653	883	10.1	–1 943
Germany	–72	145	135	5.5	351	599	256	983	1 144	643	827	107	614	7.0	–14
Ireland	11	2	14	0.6	11	7	21	12	22	339	2 060	310	348	4.0	–9
Italy	9	22	5	0.2	6	7	9	15	19	113	46	4	27	0.3	202
Netherlands	31	65	60	2.4	93	112	11	113	5 284	559	257	888	915	10.4	709
Portugal	3	4	11	0.4	12	8	20	34	44	34	480	352	123	1.4	–150
Spain	–4	7	12	0.5	247	65	506	210	150	214	579	509	310	3.5	185
United Kingdom	82	–97	370	15.0	501	940	1 364	1 233	3 229	1 866	1 279	4 210	1 828	20.9	1 219
Other Europe	163	–374	134	5.4	334	822	446	462	1 675	1 705	2 905	3 783	1 517	17.3	5 387
Nordic countries[1]	111	–413	110	4.5	205	660	316	459	893	1 378	2 757	3 735	1 300	14.8	4 517
Switzerland	36	37	17	0.7	114	134	96	–26	765	291	137	8	190	2.2	759
North America	263	795	1 024	41.5	632	1 933	636	1 319	769	853	2 433	995	1 196	13.7	2 920
Canada	33	23	27	1.1	25	8	4	87	116	150	1 999	68	307	3.5	134
USA	230	772	997	40.4	607	1 925	632	1 232	653	703	434	927	889	10.1	2 786
Other OECD countries	–9	61	51	2.1	145	129	47	259	92	266	265	272	184	2.1	155
Japan	–13	15	4	0.2	9	70	48	177	33	187	154	248	116	1.3	166
NON OECD AREA	55	162	489	19.8	201	210	638	190	915	351	1 070	489	508	5.8	895
Africa	27	–9	14	0.6	14	114	28	22	21	10	–2	4	26	0.3	–4
Central and Eastern Europe	..	..	7	0.3	–	1	17	9	19	10	59	103	27	0.3	340
Latin America-Caribbean	44	166	370	15.0	121	–3	310	50	–37	69	67	148	91	1.0	143
South and East Asia	–40	33	94	3.8	71	94	176	95	645	147	936	210	297	3.4	–76
DAEs[2]	..	..	81	3.3	71	93	175	52	638	95	881	159	271	3.1	–167
Other Asia	–40	33	13	0.5	–	1	1	43	7	52	55	51	26	0.3	91
Other countries[3]	24	–28	4	0.2	–5	4	107	14	267	115	10	24	67	0.8	492
TOTAL	596	934	2 465	100.0	2 699	5 224	4 227	5 289	16 025	10 012	13 113	13 502	8 761	100.0	8 171

1. Including Scandinavian Airline System's investments in Denmark.
2. Including Philippines.
3. Including the European countries Gibraltar, Andorra, Malta and Cyprus.
Source: Danmarks Nationalbank.

the stock figures at the end of 1991 (Europe 75 per cent, EEC 57 per cent – see Annex 3, Table 2).

During the 1985-1992 period, the main destinations for Danish investment abroad were the United Kingdom (21 per cent), Nordic countries (15 per cent) and notably (Sweden 11 per cent), France and the Netherlands (10 per cent each), and Germany (7 per cent). In 1993 however, outflows to Germany, France and Belgium-Luxembourg slipped considerably as a result of recessionary economic conditions in these countries (see Table 5).

In addition, Danish firms participated in the US inward investment boom in the second half of the eighties. The United States accounted for 13 per cent of Denmark's outward flows between 1985 and 1993 and 8 per cent of Denmark's outward stock at the end of 1991 (see Annex 3, Table 2). A record high was set in 1986 (36 per cent). The United States remained, however, the only major non-European destination of Danish outward direct investment. Some fresh investments were made in Central and Eastern Europe although at a still modest scale (0.7 per cent between 1985 and 1993).

As with inward direct investment, most outward direct investment from 1985-1993 related to the services sector (68 per cent) (Table 6), and in particular finance, insurance and business services (31 per cent), wholesale and retail trade (22 per cent) and transport and storage (5 per cent). The increased presence of Danish banks abroad is to be viewed against the continuing foreign borrowing requirements of Danish firms and their desire to take advantage of the single market. Some of these investments proved to be not very profitable, however, and were repatriated in 1993.

Manufacturing was also a significant outlet (27 per cent) during the same period. This was mainly attributed to food, beverages and tobacco (10 per cent) which comprise some of Denmark's largest industrial groups including Carlsberg, Danisco and the East Asian Company. Chemical products (5 per cent) and partly the medical firm Novo-Nordisk, also made significant inroads abroad. Large sums were invested in mechanical equipment (9 per cent) in 1992-1993. But only 4 per cent of the total was invested in the foreign primary sector.

Food, beverage and tobacco and services appear among the strongholds of the Danish economy that have recently identified by the Danish government.[9] Another indicator of Denmark's international competitive position are the

Table 6. **Direct investment flows abroad by industry, 1982-1993**[1]

DKr million

	82-87 average	% of total	88-93 average	% of total	1985	1986	1987	1988	1989	1990	1991	1992	1993
PRIMARY	30	1.1	572	5.2	18	77	65	76	94	60	2 481	82	639
SECONDARY	833	31.0	3 855	35.0	1 077	1 707	920	2 215	2 325	1 990	3 206	5 713	7 682
Food, beverages and tobacco	348	12.9	1 452	13.2	490	621	669	321	232	242	1 476	2 679	3 759
Textiles, leather and clothing	11	0.4	10	0.1	22	-72	-49	28	-3	12	25	:	:
Paper, printing and publishing	49	1.8	78	0.7	112	43	53	37	133	218	80	:	:
Chemical products	64	2.4	847	7.7	96	382	88	610	224	501	409	1 308	2 027
Coal and petroleum products	29	1.1	129	1.2	19	129	90	223	175	331	44	:	:
Non-metallic products	25	0.9	123	1.1	-6	58	13	132	751	-373	227	:	:
Metal products	22	0.8	43	0.4	-19	6	9	47	32	12	169	:	:
Mechanical equipment	227	8.4	604	5.5	355	297	128	434	485	716	125	915	948
Electric and electronic equipment	69	2.6	89	0.8	39	276	-71	92	102	190	74	-67	143
Other transport equipment	2	0.1	62	0.6	4	2	1	4	28	:	339	:	:
Other manufacturing	-12	-0.5	419	3.8	-35	-35	-11	287	166	141	238	878	805
TERTIARY	1 829	67.9	6 525	59.2	1 603	3 440	3 243	2 997	13 603	7 961	7 225	7 509	-148
Construction	130	4.8	142	1.3	176	138	162	119	307	360	67	:	:
Wholesale and retail trade	725	26.9	2 519	22.9	482	1 085	1 613	1 616	1 998	3 408	2 339	2 814	2 940.
Transport and storage	277	10.3	496	4.5	290	290	461	202	1 732	189	137	388	328
Finance, insurance and business services	439	16.3	2 565	23.3	643	1 102	307	901	5 723	3 805	4 669	4 219	-3 926
Communication	:	:	:	:	:	:	:	:	:	:	:	:	:
Other services	258	9.6	802	7.3	12	825	700	159	3 843	199	13	88	510
UNALLOCATED	:	:	67	0.6	:	:	:	:	:	:	205	198	-2
TOTAL	2 691	100.0	11 019	100.0	2 698	5 224	4 228	5 288	16 022	10 011	13 117	13 502	8 171

1. The distribution by sector concerns the company in which investment is made. In certain cases the distribution by sector is estimated for the period 1983 to 1988.
Source: Danmarks Nationalbank.

changes in the gross industry balance of outward direct investment to be observed between 1982-1987 and 1988-1993 periods (see Tables 4 and 6). Food and beverage, finance and chemicals also come out favourably from this comparison. Electric and electronic equipment, non-metallic products and transport and storage, are clearly net recipients of international direct investment.

Chapter 3

Denmark's policies toward foreign direct investment

Denmark's receptivity to overseas private direct investment is part of its tradition of non-intervention in the business sector, where it has preferred to leave the allocation of resources mostly to market forces. Economic policy has aimed at improving macroeconomic performance and instituting structural reforms that would facilitate overall growth. There has been a recognition in recent years, however, that although macroeconomic and structural policies have been important in improving Denmark's competitive position, the Danish economy's capacity to create jobs and improve competitiveness also depends on the business environment. The Danish government is therefore supplementing macroeconomic and structural policies with an industrial policy.[10]

The new industrial policy will affect the business climate generally, but may also have implications for foreign investors. For example, the government intends to play a more active role in fostering competitive advantage in certain "national strongholds", where it is felt Danish firms are internationally competitive, but where the government would like to see more foreign investment because of the new technologies and know-how that foreign firms can bring. Any improvement in the framework conditions benefits that result from the strongholds policy will therefore be made available to foreign investors on the same basis as Danish firms, but there will be no special incentives for foreign investors.

A number of market access issues are also being addressed that will affect the investment environment in Denmark, including the sale of shares in public enterprises, demonopolisation and improving competition law and practice. On demonopolisation, the government is motivated in part by EC rules on liberalisation of the internal market. The impact of these liberalisations on non-EC investors remains uncertain, however, as reciprocity may be applied to non-EC applicants wishing to participate in newly-liberalised activities such as electricity and natural gas, and oil and gas exploration and production. Liberalisations in recent years in the air and road transport sectors and in commercial fishing have also increased EC investors' access to these activities. Improvements in competition policy should make it easier for new firms, including foreign firms, to enter markets in accounting, law, advertising, construction, transportation and trade, where competition has so far been limited.

A.   Denmark's industrial policy and its impact on foreign investment

i)   Historical overview

Denmark has traditionally not had what could be called an industrial policy. Economic policy has aimed at improving overall macroeconomic performance and instituting structural reforms that would facilitate overall growth. Efforts to improve competition policy and practice and the functioning of the labour markets have been particularly important elements in structural reform policies, although rigidities in these two areas may still impede industrial development and unemployment remains a persistent problem.

Nevertheless, significant macroeconomic and structural improvements have been made in recent years which have allowed the Danish authorities to focus more specifically on industrial policy. In the past, improvements in the business environment was not an explicit policy objective, and direct support to industry remains very modest. In fact, government support to industry in Denmark is low by EC and international standards. The overall amount of state aid going to business is about 1 per cent of GDP,[11] and from 1988-1990 government support amounted to about 2 per cent of value-added in manufacturing. Except for public transportation, fishing and shipbuilding, virtually no direct support is given to the business sector.

Denmark has mostly avoided subsidising select industries, partly because it has relatively few of the traditional industries, such as automobiles and basic metals, where pressures to protect domestic firms are greatest. Support to individual firms – either to promote growth and improve competitiveness or to restructure enterprises that are troubled – is limited in Denmark. Indeed, when Denmark's dominant company in the Danish computer and microelectronics industry needed financial restructuring in the mid-1980s, the government preferred to let foreign competitors take over most of the company rather than to inject public funds. Shipbuilding and fishing are the only industries receiving substantial direct government support, although there are also a number of important subsidies in the housing market.

Most support has concentrated on improving the general conditions for business growth through policies or programmes aimed at improving infrastructure and exports, promoting R&D and stimulating risk-taking. In 1992 about 30 per cent of government support for business went to export support, almost 25 per cent went to R&D, and 16 per cent went to specific sectors. Local government authorities have assumed a relatively active role in supporting various business activities, but this has involved little budgetary cost.

Most export support has focused on government guarantees for credits to buyers of Danish exports, advice and assistance. In recent years this support has been extended to support sales and investment in Central and Eastern Europe. Export guarantees and assistance are available to all firms, not just Danish companies.

Research and development support has been small compared to other OECD countries, and government financing for private sector R&D is among the lowest in the OECD. Moreover, most government-sponsored R&D programmes require the beneficiary to pay back some of the support funds if the scheme is commercially successful. Denmark's R&D support has traditionally gone to providing technological infrastructure and programme-related services to individual companies for initiatives in favoured fields, which have included energy conservation, the environment, construction, material technologies and technologies related to food and beverages. The government has also tried to help small and medium sized companies develop and use new technologies through a network of technological institutes, and has also subsidised the creation of "industrial networks" to encourage firms to engage in joint projects. Some 2 000 to 2 500 companies are estimated to have been involved in these networks, although many were engaged in exports and marketing rather than R&D.

ii) Denmark's industrial policy

The Danish government has reexamined its business support measures in the context of a broader approach to industrial development. The Danish authorities feel that macroeconomic stability now needs to be supplemented by market-oriented industrial policy.[12] This industrial policy, which has been outlined in the 1993 business policy report, *Erhvervsredegorelse*, is broadly defined to include infrastructure, market efficiency, education and public-private interaction. Beyond these general areas, the new industrial policy has also identified five other areas where government support will concentrate. Policy measures that enhance framework conditions in those areas can be exploited by loans, grants and tax incentives, which will be offered to established foreign-controlled enterprises on the same terms and conditions as Danish and European investors. The policy does not envisage increasing the present low level of state aid to industry, however. The five areas targeted for special attention by the Danish government are:

- *a)* foreign direct investment;
- *b)* "national strongholds";
- *c)* large firms engaged in exporting;
- *d)* selected service industries;
- *e)* new and small firms.

Foreign direct investment support

Denmark's position as home and host to foreign direct investment is characterised by the relatively small amounts of direct investment going in and out of the country. Notwithstanding the increases in inward FDI in recent years, Denmark has received relatively little foreign direct investment, both in the aggregate and in relation to GDP as compared to OECD countries of comparable size. This has led to concerns that Denmark has been slow to take advantage of the international dispersion of capital, technology and management expertise that FDI facilitates. The Danish authorities have therefore identified FDI promotion as an important element in their new industrial policy. No special incentives will be offered to foreign investors, however, as the Danish government feels that macroeconomic stability, and Denmark's resource base are sufficient inducements for foreign investors. Moreover, efforts have been made to deregulate markets and make them more competitive, providing greater opportunities for foreign investors.

A key element of FDI promotion is to improve the Danish business environment in general – also the overriding objective of the entire industrial policy. Efforts to improve education, training and entrepreneurial skills are particularly important, as are efforts to enhance the competitive environment by opening restricted activities to more competition, including foreign competition.

Another central task of FDI promotion under the new industrial policy is to inform investors about specific business areas in Denmark. These areas may include some of the "stronghold areas", including sea transport, health/medical, food processing, woods and furniture, where foreign investors can benefit from special knowledge and skills in the Danish market. Indeed, the Invest in Denmark programme is entering a new, more focused phase. Rather than launching general public image campaigns, the government is placing more emphasis on analysing which kinds of foreign investment will benefit most from the Danish business environment and contribute most to its improvement. Danish embassies and consulates coordinate investment promotion abroad, holding seminars, interviews and meetings with companies, and emphasising competitive sectors in Denmark and in the home country.

A programme to promote foreign investment in Denmark has been in place since 1989, but it has not met with as much success as the Danish authorities would have liked. It targeted high-tech industries in the United States and Japan, and today has expanded to other countries, notably the United Kingdom and France. The new campaign is trying to attract to Denmark a share of the large investment projects that multinational firms are expected to place in Europe following the completion of the internal market.

A "one stop shop" for foreign investors is currently under construction. In close cooperation with local government, organisations and Danish companies, the one stop shop is supposed to provide the best possible service for visiting companies. Pilot projects in sectors that are important to Denmark's competitive position are also being launched in cooperation with the Danish business community. The aim is to attract foreign companies in industries that are important suppliers to competitive Danish firms and build links between the companies and the suppliers.

Corporate taxation has been reduced to OECD averages in recent years, but personal income taxes remain high. One incentive recently adopted gives expatriates working in Denmark the possibility of a 30 per cent income tax under certain conditions. No other special tax incentives exist for foreign investors, as existing incentives apply equally to both Danish and foreign-owned companies.

Support for national strongholds

The Danish authorities have identified ''stronghold'' areas where they feel Danish firms hold internationally competitive positions as evidenced by high productivity and profits, growing market shares and extensive foreign operations. The basis for identifying these strongholds is an analysis by the Danish Agency for the Development of Trade and Industry, where ''resource fields'' were named that were seen to deserve special attention, and where a number of mutually-supportive firms had accumulated specialised knowledge. The resource fields from which strongholds are likely to be identified are food and food processing, housing and construction, health and medicine, transport and communications, consumer goods, tourism and leisure, energy and environment and services.

Maintaining and strengthening these ''strongholds'' is an important aspect of the new approach to industrial policy. The Government plans to increase support for public infrastructure – including transportation, communications, education and research – in order to help the national strongholds that have been identified. In addition, the Danish government feels that national strongholds must be provided with general conditions which are at least as good as those of foreign competitors, but is not prepared to offer matching subsidies.

The Danish authorities distinguish between targeting competitive strongholds and ''picking winners'' by saying the former is based on past performance while the latter involves assessing various industries' future prospects. Denmark's support for ''stronghold'' industries suggests a more active and interventionist approach to industrial development, and there are concerns about the inherent resource-distorting risks associated with this approach. Moreover, it is suggested that further improvements in economic policies governing the job market, taxation and competition policy would do more to strengthen Denmark's economy than targeting stronghold areas for government attention and support.

The stronghold approach is also likely to involve more extensive and direct public involvement in research and product development in select areas. Incentives are available, for example, for the use of wind energy and solar energy, and the government offers a 30 per cent discount on the purchase of solar energy equipment. This incentive scheme, which has promoted the development of new technologies, makes no distinction between the manufacturing firms' ownership. In addition, Denmark participates in a number of European technology programmes. Currently, more than 250 private companies and public research institutes in Denmark participate in European technology programmes such as ESPRIT, EUREKA, BRITE and RACE, with participation from non-European-owned companies like AT&T and Motorola.

Support for large firms engaged in exporting

Denmark has relatively few large companies, even for a country its size. There are only about 30 companies in Denmark which employ over 2 000 people and have a foreign turnover greater than 1 billion DKr. One study found that among the Nordic countries in 1992 no Danish corporation was in the top 15 in terms of sales and employment.[13] The Danish government has stated that a desirable objective of industrial policy would be to increase the number of large firms in Denmark, in part because of their potential contribution to employment and wealth creation, and because of their favourable effect on subcontractors and other suppliers. Moreover, a substantial share of private research and development in Denmark is carried out by large firms, and the Danish authorities would like to see more R&D undertaken there.

Notwithstanding the desire to bring in more large companies, the Danish authorities see the small number of large firms as offering some advantages. For example, a small number of firms offers good opportunities for close cooperation between business and government. As part of the industrial policy, the Government is establishing a business-government dialogue to discuss public infrastructure, research, education and other matters of concern to business. The idea is to design support services in a way that is favourable to enterprises without engaging in favouritism. Some concern has been expressed about how the Danish Government intends to cooperate with the few large firms already in Denmark, and in particular, whether there is a possible risk of favouring already-established firms at the expense of those wishing to enter the Danish market. The Danish authorities have explained that cooperation will take the form of a dialogue only, and that no special incentives or other benefits will be given as a result of the dialogue.

Another element in the effort to help develop more, better and bigger firms is public procurement policies, where the government will try to raise the quality of companies' products by acting as a quality-minded customer. New technologies will also be promoted through government development contracts, where public sector suppliers will be required to develop new products that can be sold on the market. Indeed, the government will strategically contract public sector tasks and products which can be exploited commercially. Finally, the public sector itself will enter into export joint ventures with private firms in fields where it possesses specific know-how, as in social services activities.

Support to service industries

Denmark exports services – mostly business services – that correspond to around 10 per cent of its GDP, which is high even for an OECD country. The Danish authorities would nevertheless like to see service exports expand, and are trying to improve the business environment for services industries. More particularly, it is hoped that a number of service companies, many of which are related to the welfare system, will be able to expand their exports, partly in cooperation with the public sector. The Danish authorities believe that the public sector has accumulated a great deal of knowledge of potential commercial value, especially in welfare activities like hospitals, education, etc., and that the commercial potential can best be exploited through public-private cooperation in these areas.

Local governmental authorities have taken a rather active role in supporting various business activities. In fact, local authorities' business development activities have contrasted with the central government's tradition of non-interventionism, and a number of local officials have promoted special categories of business activity (for example, tourism) as well as exports and contacts with EC Members. Regulations restricting local authorities' ability to participate in business activities have been relaxed recently, so that they can now, for example, invest in firms that commercialise their expertise, as in old age homes, kindergartens or hospitals. There is neither the intention nor the political will, however, to privatise welfare activities, but rather a willingness to make these services available on a profit-making basis to customers in other countries, particularly in the Baltic states.

Support for new and small firms

Denmark's private sector has a high proportion of small and medium-sized firms compared with many other European countries. The business sector's contribution to total value-added and employment in Denmark is lower than in most OECD countries, which has been the source of some concern. The low rate of new business formation and the high rate of start-up failures has been a related concern. Some of the biggest problems impeding new business creation in Denmark, according to the Danish authorities, have been the scarce supply of venture capital, the small size of the Danish market and the need for managerial expertise in new companies. To address the financing problem, the Danish government offers guarantees to private financial institutions for up to 50 per cent of loans committed to new companies or activities. Financial institutions and pension funds may also establish venture capital institutes which will be eligible for government guarantees of up to 50 per cent of capital committed to small and medium-sized enterprises. And the government will also subsidise the cost of legal advice, accounting, and market information services for potential entrepreneurs.

It has been pointed out that while these are all important in addressing the financing shortfall for small and medium-sized enterprises, a number of other measures could be taken that would facilitate the flow of capital to nascent enterprises and enhance the rate of new business start-ups. Removing the restrictions on lending to companies not listed on the Copenhagen stock exchange, for example, may reduce impediments to small business financing.

B. Privatisation

The Danish Government has been directly involved in some commercial activities, but most government equity holdings in incorporated companies have related to public utilities in the energy and transport sectors. In comparison to some other Scandinavian neighbour governments, several of which have extensive holdings in steel, automobile and aircraft companies, for example, Denmark's state ownership in the commercial sector has been small. The Danish authorities have recognised, however, that although the government's role in the productive economy has not been large, there are still a number of areas where market access is limited and where further liberalisation could lead to greater efficiency. Starting in 1990 several state enterprises (which are mainly in the girobank, telecommunications, transport and energy sectors) have been transformed into limited liability companies in order to increase management efficiency. And a number of privatisations have already taken place or are in progress.

Privatisation in Denmark has attracted considerable political attention since the mid-1980s. The former conservative government embarked on a wide-ranging privatisation programme that was regarded as beneficial in its own right. The government wanted to reduce the state's financial commitments in the companies being privatised, raise capital to strengthen the state's budgetary position, and improve the efficiency of firms being sold. Privatisation was seen as the most effective way to do this. Not all of Denmark's political parties have been in favour of the privatisation concept, however. The new government that took office in January 1992 did not consider privatisation as a comprehensive process, and its policy has been to consider selling state assets on a case-by-case basis. The major motivations underlying the new government's ''rescheduling'' or ''corporatisation'' of state enterprises in Denmark has been to improve their competitiveness by allowing them to operate on a more commercial basis. The new government is not planning wholesale privatisation of its assets. Mogens Lykketoft, the Minister of Finance, has said that ''the Danish state is not planning to sell the majority of the shares'' in utilities or other state services that have been set up as limited companies. There remains the possibility, however, that some activities might be further opened to private participation, as in local bus and ferry transportation, and certain postal services.

The Ministry of Finance is the co-ordinator of the detailed planning and execution of privatisations in Denmark. The sale of shares in government-owned companies is carried out either as a public offering or as a private placement. Sometimes the entire share capital is sold, while at other times the government retains a majority or minority holding in the company. As a rule there are no limitations on the number of shares each investor may hold in a state-owned company, although it is possible to incorporate specific provisions in the law which limit the number of shares an individual investor may hold after the privatisation, and/or preventing certain investors from acquiring shares in the company.

The Danish authorities have elected to keep a majority share ownership in a number of privatisations that have occurred, rather than maintaining a "golden share" or selecting "core shareholders," as in some other OECD countries. The reason has been a desire to maintain control over important strategic decisions which could affect basic infrastructure and services. The Danish authorities, maintain, however, that privatised firms will have operational independence, and that the state will act commercially in its decisions as majority shareholder.

The first major privatisation to take place in Denmark was the sale of the State Life Insurance Company (now Danica) to the Baltica Insurance Company, a Danish firm, in 1990.[14] After a public offering with announcements in the international financial press, the government negociated with five or six conforms before selecting the buyer. The sale was made as a private placement in which the entire share capital was acquired by Baltica after negotiations between a limited number of bidders. Between 1990 and 1992 a number of other state enterprises were transformed into 100 per cent state-owned public limited companies, some of whose shares were then offered publicly. Among these were the Copenhagen airport, the telephone companies, an export credit insurance company (EKR), the postal bank (GiroBank), and the state data company (DataCentralen). Fifty per cent of the shares in Dan Computer Management, a subsidiary of DataCentralen were sold to a strategic partner, Maersk Data, an affiliate of the large Danish shipping company. The sale of 51 per cent of the shares in GiroBank was made through a public offering on the Copenhagen stock exchange.

In recent months the state has sold some of its interests in the Copenhagen airports and in Tele Danmark, the state telecommunications company. In the Copenhagen airports sale, which includes Copenhagen's international Kastrup airport and the Tune airport between the capital and the nearby town of Roskilde, the state sold a 25 per cent share of its 100 per cent holdings by public international offering. No discrimination was made between investors in Denmark and elsewhere.

The Tele Danmark privatisation is particularly important. Tele Danmark is the first in a succession of planned telecommunications privatisations in the European Community, and its success will therefore have a bearing on others. It is the largest share offering ever made on the Copenhagen exchange and globally has attracted very significant attention from both local and international investors. Indeed, many foreign investors who had not invested in Danish shares before may now look anew to the Danish market. Unusually for a telecommunications privatisation, nearly all of the net proceeds will go to the company, not to the government (out of a total revenue of 19 billion DKr, the government secured 0.9 billion DKr).

Tele Danmark is the principal provider of domestic and international telephone services in Denmark, and the sole provider of leased lines there. In addition, it is one of two operators of public mobile telephone services and is also engaged in the supply and service of telecommunications equipment, data communications services and cable television. Tele Danmark operates under a concession from the Danish government granting it an exclusive right to provide in Denmark the following:

- Telephone services, text and data communication services, permanent leased lines, mobile communication and satellite services, and broadcasting through the telecommunications network of radio and television programmes.
- Tele Danmark also has an exclusive right on the telecommunications infrastructure, which includes infrastructure and services exclusively for its own use. Further, this exclusive right is extended by Executive Order to internal networks.

The Danish government will retain a controlling 51 per cent stake in Tele Danmark, but the company will have operational independence. Indeed, a major motivation behind the decision to privatise was to enable the company to stay competitive in the face of increasing competition. Tele Danmark's chief executive, Hans Wurzen, has said privatisation would enable the company ''to move away from political control in the face of competition in an open market in Europe''.[15] The company's articles of association stipulate that no shareholder except the state may own more than 7.5 per cent of the share capital, but that in certain circumstances the board of directors may accept a higher level of ownership, *e.g.* to a strategic partner. The sale of shares has been divided into different tranches, with some 41 per cent going to the American market, 20 per cent to the Nordic market, 16 per cent to the United Kingdom, 14 per cent to the rest of Europe and 9 per cent to the rest of the world. Employees of the company and its subsidiaries were also given the right to purchase shares at a favourable price, and part of the Nordic tranche was offered to Danish retail investors prior to the global offer. Otherwise, no discrimination was made between investors in Denmark and in the rest of the world.

C.   Liberalisation of concessions and monopolies

A number of public regulations have distorted competitive forces in several sectors in Denmark, as in other OECD countries, and the Danish authorities are taking steps to remove or reduce barriers to entry and operation in several of these areas. Legal barriers to competition have been reduced, for example, in telecommunications and postal services, and the Giro bank's statutory monopoly on handling state payments has been abolished. Entry barriers are still present in the operation of telecom-network and exchange station operations, letter mail services, rail traffic, electricity network operations and the sale and transportation of natural gas. Concessions are required for energy and water distribution and waste disposal, and authorisations for entry are used extensively in health services and the professional services.

There is no single policy governing the way concessions are granted to engage in various sectors and activities in Denmark. Each ministry sets its own guidelines according to legal and technical criteria applicable to the activity for which the concession is being granted, and in accordance with EC laws. As a general rule, however, concessions are granted on a non-discriminatory basis to domestic and foreign investors, and EC and non-EC investors are treated alike. Concessions may be granted to incorporated firms and to branches, and investors are generally free to choose the form of establishment.

i)   Telecommunications

The Danish Ministry for Communications and Tourism has responsibility for the regulation of the telecommunications sector in Denmark. The Minister has delegated most regulatory functions to Telestyrelsen, following the 1994 amendment to the Telecommunications Act of 1990. Regulation of Denmark's telecommunications sector is governed by two basic laws: the Telegraphs and Telephones Act of 1897, as amended, and the 1990 Act, as modified most recently by the 1994 Amendment. This legislation (and the related 1990 Political Agreement), the Concession, and certain other executive orders and guidelines issued by the Minister for Communications and Tourism make up the basic elements of the telecommunications regulatory framework in Denmark.[16] The regulatory regime must comply with European Union legislation.

In June 1993 and February 1994, two supplements to the 1990 Political Agreement were adopted that set forth a plan for further liberalising the telecommunications sector in Denmark. On 9 February 1994, a Bill to implement the Political Agreement and amend the Telecommunications Act 1990 was introduced, which authorized the Minister to liberalize some telecommunications services. This authorization has been applied for the liberalization of data communication services, provision of services in the premium rate series, and provision of public pay-phone services. The telecommunications infrastructure will be liberalized when the European Commission's *Green Paper* on infrastructure has been finalized.

Telecommunications services liberalisation will effectively widen the network's field of application, and will be organized as follows:

– during the first six months of 1994, rules governing access to permanent leased lines for telephony will be relaxed. This liberalization will come into effect by way of an amendment of the Telecommunications Act 1990;
– in 1994 competition will be introduced for the digital public paging service, ERMES, and for use of DECT technology in public telecommunications services. Separate legislation will be prepared to cover liberalisation of these fields;
– in 1994 competition will be introduced for satellite services. Existing legislation will be used for this liberalisation;
– further liberalization is planned between now and 1 March 1997, which will be subject to agreement between the political parties to the above-mentioned political agreement of 22 June 1990.

The liberalisation described above will effectively curtail the state's exclusive right of telephony services. This means that service providers other than Tele Danmark will gain access to permanent leased lines and be able to provide services to third parties. Moreover, the introduction of separate legislation covering ERMES and DECT will lead to a curtailment of the concession held by Tele Danmark. Licenses for mobile and digital telecommunications services will be limited, but foreign firms, both those inside and outside the EC, will be given the same access to licenses as Danish enterprises. Some foreign firms already participate in alternative telecommunications services in Denmark: the US telecommunications company, Bell South, owns 30 per cent of a competing firm engaged in mobile services in Denmark, for example.

The liberalisation of telecommunications services has been given high priority in Denmark. The Danish authorities believe that by preserving the public telecommunications infrastructure as a reserved area, service providers in the newly-liberalized area will be ensured equal and uniform conditions for using the public telecommunications infrastructure. Foreign firms will be given the same opportunity to access permanent leased lines as Danish companies, and EC and non-EC firms will be treated alike. In fact, American Telephone and Telegraph (AT&T) and British Telecommunications (BT) have already bid for access to the leased line network.

ii) Energy

Electricity

Electricity supply activities in Denmark are regulated according to the Electricity Supply Act of 25 February 1976. According to this Act, electricity supply activities from production plants with a capacity of more than 25 megawatt or from transmission or distribution plants constructed for tensions over 100 kV may be operated only by authorisation granted by the Ministry of Energy. Such authorisation cannot be granted for a shorter period than 20 years [article 3(1)]. Electricity supplying undertakings which only distribute electricity do not need an authorisation [article 3(2)].

Natural Gas

According to the Natural Gas Supply Act of 10 June 1972, natural gas may be imported, sold, transported or stored only in accordance with an authorization or concession from the Ministry of Energy, which is granted in the form of a sole rights concession (article 1). The state-owned company, DANGAS, obtained the authorization as a sole rights concession in 1979. The distribution is carried out by five regional companies owned by the municipalities.

On 24 February 1992 the European Commission forwarded to the Council proposals for Council Directives concerning common rules for the internal market in electricity and natural gas. The opinion of the Parliament was delivered on 17 November 1993, and in December 1993 the Commission presented amended proposals for Council Directives. These proposals would open up the energy market, make greater integration of the gas and electricity markets in the Community, and create greater competitiveness among Community companies.

The proposal concerning common rules for the internal market in natural gas is intended to establish common rules for storage, transmission and distribution of natural gas. It lays down the organisational and operating arrangements for the natural gas sector, access to the market, criteria an procedures applicable to the granting of licences for transmission, storage, distribution and supply of natural gas, and for system operation.

DANGAS has already given up its sole right to import natural gas, and under an EC proposed Council directive it would appear that DANGAS may also have to surrender its exclusive rights to sell, transport and store natural gas as well. Indeed, this decision has already been taken in principle, and would be implemented in the context of EC negotiations on the single market for natural gas. In the event DANGAS' exclusive rights are surrendered, it is envisaged that non-discriminatory rules would apply, and that Danish and non-Danish investors would be treated equally.

The Danish Government is exploring the need for changes in the Danish energy sector in the light of the negotiations on an internal energy market.

Oil and gas exploration and production

Exploration and production of oil and gas in Denmark can only be carried out in accordance with 2a license issued by the Ministry of Energy. A license may be granted in the form of a non-exclusive permit to perform specific types of initial surveys, or as exclusive concessions to explore and produce hydrocarbons. Permits and concessions are issued pursuant to the Subsoil Act of 10 June 1981, and are granted on the basis of non-discriminatory criteria published in the public call for applications. Exclusive concessions are a precondition for achieving private financing of exploration and production of oil and gas.

On 11 May 1992 the European Commission proposed a Council Directive on the conditions for granting and using authorisations for the prospection, exploration and production of hydrocarbons. On 22 December 1993 the Council adopted a common position on the proposal, which is scheduled to come into force by July 1995. Article 8 of the Directive contains a reciprocity provision in which the Commission may seek a negotiating mandate from the Council to obtain comparable competitive opportunities for Community entities that are not receiving from third countries treatment comparable to that which the Community grants entities from that third country.

The Danish authorities are encouraging direct foreign investment in the oil and gas exploration sector, and do not intend to press for reciprocity when granting concessions in this sector. There is no discrimination on granting a license but non-EC companies are required to establish a branch or a subsidiary in Denmark, primarily for tax purposes.

iii) Postal services

The Post Office, which is owned and operated by the Danish State, is under the competence of the Minister for Communication and Tourism, and is managed by a Director General who is in charge of operations and new installations. In a formal sense, the Post Office was not established as a state enterprise but it has obligations normally associated with state enterprises. For example, it is under obligation to maintain a universal service that provides the public with day-to-day delivery of ordinary postal items at affordable and uniform prices.

The Post Office has an exclusive right to collect, transmit and deliver addressed letters (reserved service). This applies to both inland letters and letters to and from abroad. The Post Office may also offer other services, too, by a provision which allows it greater flexibility to pursue commercial activities.

Developments in the EC are causing national administrations to gradually adapt to changing circumstances in postal services. The EC *Green Paper* and Council Resolution on the liberalisation of European postal services suggest that postal services liberalisation will be undertaken in the future. There is agreement at the EC level, however, that some degree of exclusive right (reserved service) should be reserved in return for maintaining universal service. Further, it is likely that the EC will require regulatory and operational functions to be separate. These new rules on postal services in the EC will necessitate far-reaching amendments of the Post Office Act.

The Danish authorities feel that it is necessary that the Post Office be given more commercial freedom to introduce new services as customers' demands change, and more operational flexibility may be needed to compete with private undertakings.

It is expected that the State's exclusive right of transmission of addressed letters will be maintained in return for upholding the state's obligation to transmit universally. Moreover, it is assumed that the Minister for Communications and Tourism will be authorised to stipulate the extent of reserved and universal services by fixing weight limits, price limits and physical measurements. Further, the Minister will be given the possibility of setting service objectives and criteria for postal services. No position has yet been taken as to what kind of organisation the Post Office would need in order to fulfil the above requirements.

D.   Other market access issues

i)   Competition policy and private practices

The Danish authorities recognise the importance of competitive markets in maximising economic welfare, and have taken steps to strengthen the legal framework governing competition among businesses. Competition law and practice is being reviewed and strengthened in Denmark, as a number of important activities remain shielded from competition or are relatively unexposed to market pressures. In the professional services, transportation, construction and distribution sectors, anti-competitive agreements may still exist, taking the form of price lists, price-setting rules and discount allowances. These agreements may seriously weaken competition and lead to less dynamic markets. Indeed, the Danish authorities have recognised this problem, and dismantling anti-competitive agreements has been high on the competition authorities' list of priorities in recent years. Efforts here have met with some success.

Indeed, increasing competition in the Danish market is an important economic policy objective, and the government is currently working to remove entry regulations that have stifled competition in construction, transportation and trade. A new Competition Act was enacted in 1990 which strengthened the legal framework governing competition among businesses, and gave the competition authorities wide-ranging powers to obtain and disclose information about restrictive business powers. The Danish Competition Council is working to prohibit horizontal agreements on prices and market sharing, and its actions have been confirmed in appeals before the Competition Appeals Tribunal. A special committee is also studying the advantages and disadvantages of changing to the prohibition principle in Danish competition law, under which collusive arrangements are prohibited. A report will be made to the Minister of Industry by April 1995.

In addition to impediments resulting from competition law and practice, shareholding arrangements for some types of companies in Denmark may impede foreign access to those companies. These restrictive measures, which are sanctioned under Danish law, apply equally to Danish and non-Danish investors. There are two types of companies with limited liability that are regulated by law: *aktieselskaber* and *anpartsselskaber*, which are respectively very similar to the German Aktiengesellschaft (AG) and Gesellschaft mit beschränkter Haftung (GmbH). The ''shares'' in the *anpartsselskab* cannot be offered to the public in general, but this restriction applies both to Danish and foreign investors. Moreover, the acts concerning *aktieselskaber* and *anpartsselskaber* do not distinguish between Danish and foreign investors.

It is possible to have prior approval clauses and pre-emption pacts if these clauses are contained in the articles of association and the shares are nominal shares. As regards pre-emption pacts concerning the right for the company to acquire shares, the board can be authorized by the general meeting to acquire up to 10 per cent of the company's shares. It is not possible, however, for the board to have a general authorization to acquire company shares.

An *aktieselskab* company is allowed to acquire up to 10 per cent of its own issued shares, but this must be authorised in a general meeting. There may be instances, however, in order ''to avoid serious and threatening harm,'' where the company may acquire its own shares without authorization by a general meeting. The board must in that case inform the next general meeting. The company is not allowed to subscribe to its own shares. There are legal restrictions concerning the regulation of votes in *aktieselskaber*. All shares must be given a vote, but the voting rights of an individual shareholder may be limited.

Regarding *anpartsselskaber* there are no limitations in the Private Companies Act as to individual shareholder's voting rights, it is not obligatory to give all shares a vote, and the amount of votes exercised by the individual shareholder – regardless of the size of his stock of shares in the company – may be limited.

These kinds of private practices are accepted in Denmark, and are used to ensure stability in the composition of shareholders. Discrimination against foreign investors is not permitted, however. Direct investment prospects, for both foreign and Danish investors, could be improved then if more firms listed on the Copenhagen stock exchange. At present, many Danish firms prefer not to list on the stock exchange because they do not like the disclosure rules that listing requires, and Danish companies' reliance on loan financing is one of the highest in the OECD. This disincentive to list on the stock exchange may act as an impediment to foreign direct investment, as buying equity through the purchase of stocks is clearly an important means by which to invest in a country, including merger or takeover.

ii) Public order and national security

Denmark has no "catch-all" measure that could be broadly applied to restrict foreign investment for reasons of public order and national security. A very narrow list, which excludes equipment having no civilian application, has been established to clearly delineate the specific activities where foreign investment is limited for public order and national security reasons. Moreover, Denmark liberalised in 1990 foreign investment in war manufacturing enterprises. In short, Denmark's FDI restrictions in the national security area are very limited and have recently become even more limited.

Denmark's FDI restrictions based on public order and national security concerns are limited to the manufacture of war equipment. The 1990 War Equipment Act (No. 400) applies to the following:

- Equipment designed for military use and having no civilian application.
- Arms, apart from arms specially designed for use in hunting, sports, or like.
- Ammunition which may be used for military purposes.
- Gunpowder and explosives.
- Components and parts designed for use in equipment, etc., as mentioned above, and having no civilian application.

The rules on restriction of foreign influence in Danish enterprises apply to all states, including EC-countries, EEA-countries and the OECD-community. The Act does not apply to foodstuffs nor to know-how or similar intellectual property. The manufacture of war equipment is only allowed with the permission of the Minister of Justice, and all steps in the manufacturing process are included in this provision. However, war equipment repairs and the like do not require permission. Enterprises whose war equipment work is of minor importance, or which manufacture gunpowder or explosives only, may obtain exemption from the provisions of the Act on foreign influence.

Privately-owned enterprises may obtain permission to manufacture war equipment if the proprietor is a Danish citizen. For limited companies, cooperative societies or the like, the legal entity must be domiciled in Denmark. Furthermore, managers and persons authorised to sign for enterprises manufacturing war equipment are Danish citizens, and at least 80 per cent of the members of the board of directors must be Danish citizens.

With regard to the capital requirements of the enterprises, at least 60 per cent of the company capital must be in Danish hands, and foreigners' total share of the company capital may not exceed more than 20 per cent of the voting rights. Foreigners may not, through the possession of capital or in any other way, exert a dominant influence on an enterprise manufacturing war equipment. Enterprises manufacturing war equipment may only raise foreign loans or loans with a foreign guarantee if the enterprise has obtained consent from the Minister of Justice.

Under the previous Act (Act No. 139 of 7 May 1937 on supervision of the preparation of war equipment, etc., cf. Consolidated Act No. 626 of 15 September 1986), only enterprises that were wholly Danish-owned could get permission to manufacture war equipment, and all of the directors had to be Danish citizens. The present rules allow for limited foreign influence on war equipment manufacturing enterprises, because the Danish authorities want to improve Danish enterprises' access in the development and manufacture of war equipment, both in a NATO context and among the European NATO countries.

E. Sectoral measures

i) *Banking and financial services*

The establishment of subsidiaries in Denmark from foreign banks originating from countries outside the EEA-area will be governed by the Second Banking Co-Ordination Directive (89/646). According to this directive (Articles 8 and 9) the Danish competent authorities can suspend their decisions regarding requests for authorizations to credit institutions which directly or indirectly are owned by companies domiciled in a third country. The Danish Act on Banks and Savings Banks refers directly to the provisions in the Second Banking Co-Ordination Directive.

Denmark has long pursued very liberal policy and practices in welcoming inward direct investment in subsidiaries (and branches) from banks abroad. In fact an application for setting up a subsidiary (or branch) in Denmark has never been rejected on reciprocity grounds.

Branches from non-EEA countries and the treatment of such branches are left to purely national competence. In December 1990 Danish laws and practices in this area were adapted so that no reciprocity criteria regarding branches from OECD-countries would be applied.

ii) *Insurance*

According to the EC life insurance and non-life insurance directives, establishment of insurance companies originating in non-EC member countries may be subject to a reciprocity requirement. The reciprocity provision is included in the Danish Act on insurance. The Act is unchanged and the Danish authorities feel that they cannot yet give up the potential use of this provision. However, the administrative practice for granting authorizations is liberal and for several years no application for authorization has been turned down.

iii) *Air transport*

The right of establishment in air transport in Denmark is governed by EC Council Regulation No. 2407/92 of 23 July 1992 on licensing of air carriers, just as in the rest of the European Community. According to this regulation, EC undertakings meeting certain requirements are entitled to receive operating licenses to carry out carriage by air passengers, mail and/or cargo for remuneration or hire within the European Community. The EC Council Regulation on licensing is one of three EC Council Regulations in the so-called "third package" of liberalisation which came into effect from 1 January 1993.

The purpose of the EC regulations is to make criteria granting licenses to Community air carriers uniform in all Member States. Restrictions on cross-border investment have been removed with the entry into force of the third package, and Member States may no longer favour certain flag carriers by issuing licenses on a discretionary basis, at least insofar as EC carriers are concerned. Any airline which meets uniform financial safety and nationality requirements is entitled to an operating licence in any Member State where it is based.

One of the requirements is that the undertaking shall be continuously owned, directly or through majority ownership, by Member States and/or nationals of Member States. The undertaking shall be effectively controlled by such States or such nationals at all times. The undertaking's principal place of business and its registered office shall be located in the Member State issuing the licence.

According to an Air Transport Agreement concluded between the EC and Norway and Sweden, the EC-licensing Regulation – being part of the so-called third EC-liberalisation package for air transport -is also applicable in Norway and Sweden. Consequently, Norwegian and Swedish undertakings can be established as air carriers in the EC Member States under the same conditions as EC undertakings.

Up to now Denmark has accepted a maximum of 49 per cent investments by foreign investors in Danish air carriers, but after the 1 January 1995 third liberalisation package effective control by Danish or EC investors is required. Denmark will probably still accept a maximum of 49 per cent investments on the condition that the majority (51 per cent) has the effective control.

There is more than one Danish air carrier. Maersk Air I/S and DDL (Det Danske Luftfartselskab A/S), the most important players, are both Danish-owned air companies. The latter is one of the three parent companies of Scandinavian Airlines System (SAS) and is owned by 50 per cent of the Danish State. The former is owned by a single owner. The private portion of DDL's shares, including those for Sweden and Norway, is negotiable.

iv) *Road transport: passenger, freight and charter*

To obtain authorization to establish a road transport enterprise in Denmark for passengers or goods, the applicant must fulfil certain requirements concerning 1) financial soundness, 2) professional skill and 3) personal conduct in accordance with EC directives.[17] A further requirement is that the applicant must have Danish citizenship and residence in Denmark, if the enterprise is owned by the applicant. For corporate enterprises, where the enterprise is a legal person – whose owner(s) could be of any nationality – the same citizenship and residency requirements must be fulfilled by the person who is responsible for the daily management of the enterprise.

The Danish legislation on road transport for passengers and goods contains specific exemptions on Danish citizenship and residence requirements, which can be granted by international agreement or by the Minister of Transport. This exemption fulfils Denmark's obligations towards citizens from other member states of the European Community and parties to the EEA Agreement, but does not apply to other OECD Member countries.

The Danish legislation as described above contains no restrictions on foreign investments in transport enterprises in Denmark, as long as the person responsible for the daily management of the enterprise meets the requirements concerning professional skill, personal conduct, and EC or EEA citizenship, etc.

County authorities in Denmark are responsible for public bus transport, with planning undertaken by either the county authorities themselves or by a public transport enterprise established in accordance with the legislation on public transport.

Public transport in the metropolitan area is performed partly by the public transport enterprise itself and partly by private transport enterprises. Starting in 1989 the Danish government began to gradually allow private operators, under contract with the public transport enterprise, to provide passenger transport in Copenhagen. Private operators now account for approximately 45 per cent of the transport business in Copenhagen. Outside the metropolitan area public transport is generally performed by private enterprises on the basis of contracts with the public administrative transport enterprise. A ''standard contract'' has been negotiated between the private coach owners' association and the organization of the municipal authorities for this purpose.

To some extent these contracts are already used in tendering procedures, which will be obligatory from 1 July 1994, when the EC provisions concerning tendering of public services contracts come into force. As far as nationality is concerned, there are no limitations as to who can submit a tender, and all applicants are treated alike.

v) *Maritime transport*

Ownership of Danish flag vessels must be through an enterprise incorporated in Denmark. Danish citizenship is required with regard to ownership of Danish flag vessels registered in the Danish Register of Shipping or in the Danish International Register of Shipping except in the following cases:

- through part ownerships where at least two-thirds of the shipping partnership are owned by Danish subjects and the managing owner is a Danish subject resident in Denmark;
- through joint stock companies and other companies with limited liability with a board of directors where at least two-thirds of the board are Danish subjects and resident in Denmark.

Furthermore, foreign-owned vessels may be registered in the Danish International Registry of Shipping 1) where Danish citizens or companies carry on shipping activities as a significant part of their activities; 2) have a considerable direct or indirect share of the capital in the foreign company and, by virtue of the capital, a considerable degree of influence through voting rights or in other ways; and 3) provided the foreign company has an appointed representative in Denmark.

EC/EEA nationals and companies (but not investors from other OECD countries) are treated as Danish subjects in respect of ownership of Danish flag vessels, according to amendments recently adopted by the Danish parliament (Folketinget). More detailed rules are expected to be adopted shortly.

Existing regulations permitting restrictions in micro-cabotage (vessels below 500 GT) as a result of authorisation procedures applicable to foreign vessels seeking to carry out cabotage services in Danish waters had been removed on 23 July 1994.

vi)   Commercial fishing

Only individuals and companies registered with the Danish fishing authorities may fish commercially within Danish territorial waters and on Danish fishing vessels, according to the Law on Salt Water Fisheries. Companies are entitled to register with the Danish authorities, provided that two-thirds of the owners hold a registration for conducting commercial fishing. Registration is open to those who can prove previous employment as fishermen and who hold Danish citizenship, or have been resident in Denmark for at least two years. These residency/citizenship requirements, which date back from the start of this century, aim to ensure a link between the person or company utilizing the stocks and the Danish fishing industry.

Through an amendment to the Law on Salt Water Fisheries, citizens of the European Community are secured rights to practice commercial fishing in Denmark, even without meeting the Danish citizenship or residence requirements. Similar rules will be applied in order to meet the obligations under the EEA agreement. International fishing activities are also regulated within the framework of the United Nations's Convention on The Law of The Sea.

vii)   Broadcasting

The Danish Broadcasting Act (Act No. 1065 of 23 December 1992 with further amendments) sets out rules for who may provide radio and television programme services in Denmark.

The state monopoly in the broadcasting area is limited to nationwide terrestrial radio and television programmes. Satellite and cable broadcasting licences are available to any company fulfilling the (non-discriminatory) requirements laid down by regulations. Likewise, local broadcasting is open to competition. The reason for the state monopoly on nationwide terrestrial broadcasting is the scarcity of frequencies allocated to Denmark. It is of vital interests to the cultural policy of any country, including smaller countries, to be able to establish and maintain a public service broadcasting system.

1. *Danmarks Radio (DR) and Television 2 (TV 2)* are public service institutions. Danmarks Radio is financed through licence fees, and TV 2 through advertisements and licence fees. Danmarks Radio broadcasts

one nation wide TV channel and three nation wide radio channels. TV 2 broadcast 1 nationwide TV channel and 8 regional television channels.

2. *Satellite- and cable broadcasters.* Companies under Danish jurisdiction can obtain a licence to broadcast via satellite or cable (exceeding a single local area). Licences are issued by an independent Satellite and Cable Committee, which also must ensure that rules on advertisements, sponsorship, European programme quotas, etc., are observed. Advertisements are not allowed on the cable channel. Licences cannot be granted to local broadcasters or to the Danish telecommunications companies or their affiliates.

3. *Local radio and television broadcasters.* Licences are granted by local committees. Commercial companies cannot obtain a licence for local radio and television broadcasters, nor may they have a dominant influence on a station. Among the preconditions for getting a licence is that the majority of the board members must be residents of the local area in question, and the stations must have broadcasting as their sole purpose.

viii) *Gambling, betting and lotteries*

Pools, lotto, etc.

According to proclamation 637 of 27 July 1993 – the law on specific lotteries and other forms of gambling – licences to carry out gambling, lotteries and bets can be granted, when the business in question does not deal with horse, cycle, greyhound or pigeon racing, nor State lotteries, casinos or bonus savers' schemes. A Licence can only be granted to one company for a 5 year period. Only limited liability companies can obtain such a licence.

State Lottery

According to Law 235 of 8 April 1992 on the Danish State Lottery (Ltd.), the company was established with the specific purpose of carrying out the State lottery. The licence is granted for up to 10 years at a time. Other kinds of State lottery may be licensed, according to the Ministry of Justice Lottery Circular. However, such a licence can only be granted locally, and not for cash prizes. The circular is undergoing revision.

Totalizator betting (Horses)

According to proclamation 186 of 16 March 1989 – the Law on Totalizator Betting – a licence can be granted for totalizator betting and other kinds of betting. A licence is granted for up to three years at a time, or for a specific number of days within a year.

Casinos

Act No. 397 of 13 June 1990 on gambling casinos, which entered into force on 31 December 1990, provides that the Minister for Justice may grant permission to establish and operate gambling casinos. When determining whether permission may be granted, it should be emphasized, according to the Act, that the person applying for permission must be presumed to intend to operate the casino in a fully responsible manner. That is to say that the casino should be run in a financially sound matter, and that the casino should not give rise to disturbances of the peace. There are no restrictions as to who may apply for permission to establish a casino. In principle, individuals, as well as companies, foundations, associations, and the like may thus apply for permission. It is not a condition for obtaining permission to establish and operate a gambling casino in Denmark that the applicant is a Danish citizen, or that the legal entity in question is Danish-owned.

Chapter 4

Conclusions

Denmark's is an open economy and the authorities welcome foreign direct investment. Direct investment inflows have been smaller than in other OECD countries of comparable size, however, and the Danish authorities are hoping to attract larger shares of direct investment capital. There are no plans to offer foreign investors any special incentives or other inducements, as the Danish Government feels that the country's economic stability, sound public finances, and educated and productive workforce should be sufficient to attract productive private investment.

As in other EC countries, Denmark has liberalised foreign direct investment in a number of activities, partly as a result of EC directives and the EEA agreement, but it has not extended this liberalisation to all OECD investors. Investors from outside the EC or EEA may be treated differently than those from inside the Community in several important areas. There are reciprocity provisions for non-EU investors in banking and financial services and insurance; reciprocity may also be applied to non-EU investors when granting rights for oil and gas exploration and development; and the liberalisation which has taken place in air transport, maritime transport and commercial fishing vessels has not been extended to all OECD countries.

Denmark has, however, been actively seeking to increase investors' access to a number of its important markets, largely through selling shares in state enterprises, demonopolising restricted activities and improving competition law and practice. The Government's decision to sell 49 per cent of its shares in TeleDanmark and curtail its exclusive right of telephony and mobile phone services, for example, will effectively open much of the telecommunications market to new competitors in Denmark. And the sale of shares in insurance, the Giro postal bank and the Copenhagen airport have also been important. The Danish Competition Council's new powers to obtain and disclose information helps prohibit horizontal agreements on pricing and market sharing, reduce contractual barriers to competition, and open possibilities for new entrants, both Danish and foreign, in such sectors as transportation, construction and distribution.

Having made significant macroeconomic and structural improvements in recent years, the Danish authorities now regard industrial policy as necessary. The industrial policy does not envisage increasing the present low level of subsidies and support to business, but the Government has nevertheless identified several areas where they will focus their attention in an effort to improve the business climate. Foreign direct investment promotion, support for ''stronghold'' industries, and closer contact between the government and established companies are three elements of industrial policy that are particularly important to foreign investors. The Danish authorities hope to foster mutually beneficial contacts between foreign investors and Danish ''stronghold'' industries, including sea transport, health/medical, food processing, wood and furniture. The government also wants to establish a business-government dialogue to discuss public infra-structure, research and other business-related matters.

This suggests a more interventionist approach to industrial development than has been Denmark's practice in the past. In deciding how to identify and support stronghold industries, the Danish authorities need to ensure that non-resident and established foreign investors are treated like Danish firms. Likewise, the business-government dialogue on transportation, communications, education and research should include the full and equal participation of established foreign firms.

Finally, industrial development will be enhanced to the extent that markets are opened to greater competition, including foreign competition. Continued efforts are needed to strengthen competition policy, notably with respect to anti-competitive agreements. Measures aimed at removing private practices that have left some firms relatively unexposed to market pressures might also be consid-ered. Improvements in industrial competitiveness and economic welfare should be the result, with enhanced possibilities for foreign investment as well.

Notes

1. *OECD Economic Surveys: Denmark 1993-1994.*

2. Besides the Nationalbank's direct investment statistics, there are other sources publicly available. Danmarks Statistik has drawn up annual capital balance sheets, including balance-sheet figures concerning direct investment. Danmarks Statistik also prepares at intervals statistics of companies in Denmark by foreign companies. The Danish Monopolies Control Authority publishes an annual review entitled *Mergers and Company Acquisitions in Danish Industry* including the acquisition of companies in Denmark by foreign companies.

3. The liberalisation of foreign-exchange regulations on 1 October 1988 removed the prior authorisation requirement for ingoing and outgoing investments exceeding DKr 10 million. At the same time, the Nationalbank increased the details for reporting payments concerning direct investments. Enterprises are being asked to indicate in particular in the payments report whether the direct investment concerns new establishment, acquisition or extension of an investment already made; whether a contribution towards current expenses or repatriation is involved; the name, address, country and sector category as well as type of enterprise (production enterprise, sales company, etc.) for the investor as well as the enterprise to be invested; and the investor share's of the company's capital after the transaction had been made. For further explanations on Danish statistics see Danmarks Nationalbank issues of *Monetary Review* of May 1987 and November 1988.

4. Under the IMF/OECD indicative benchmark definition, foreign direct investment refers to investment that involves a long-term relationship reflecting a lasting interest of a resident entity in one economy (direct investor) in an entity resident in an economy other than that of the investor. The direct investor's purpose is to exert a significant degree of influence on the management of the enterprise resident in the other economy. This is defined as a 10 per cent or more ownership of the ordinary shares or voting power of an incorporated enterprise or the equivalent of an unincorporated enterprise. See *Detailed Benchmark Definition of Foreign Direct Investment*, OECD, 1992.

5. See Danmarks Nationalbank, *Monetary Review*, August 1994.

6. This is also true for international trade since Denmark exports and imports about 27 per cent of its GDP. The main export items are as follows: food and beverages; wood and paper; chemicals; machines and equipment; construction and tradable services (retail and wholesale, transport, financial services, business services, household services and home services).

7. It should be noted that investment from Scandinavian Airlines System are recorded as originating from Sweden where SAS headquarters are located. Shipping is also an important FDI beneficiary in this sector.

8. *Business Environment in Denmark*, Ministry for Business Policy Coordination (now merged with the Ministry of Industry and called the Ministry for Industry and Coordination), October 1993.

9. The other sectors considered to be the most competitive are health/medical, leisure/tourism, transport/communication, energy/environment, construction/housing and consumer goods. See *Business Environment in Denmark,* Ministry for Business Policy Coordination, October 1993.

10. *Business Environment in Denmark.*

11. *OECD Economic Surveys: Denmark 1993-1994,* OECD Paris.

12. *Business Environment in Denmark.*

13. "Small Country Manufacturing Industries in Transition – the Case of the Nordic region", *Working Paper No. 394,* L. Oxelheim and R. Gärtner, Industriens Utredningsinstitut, Stockholm (1993).

14. *Privatisation: A World Privatisation Guide*, International Financial Law Review Special Supplement, April 1994.

15. "Denmark Leads off Telecoms Sales with Likely $2.7bn Float,"*Financial Times,* 22 March 1994.

16. Under the 1990 Act the Minister granted to Tele Danmark the Concession, which came into effect in January 1991, and consists of an exclusive right to provide public voice telephone services, text and data communications services (except those that have been opened to competition by the Minister), leased lines, mobile communications (except certain services covered by the Mobile Act) and satellite services, and to transmit radio and television programmes through the telecommunications network. Tele Danmark was also granted the right to install and operate the public telecommunications infrastructure, described as all transmission routes and exchanges linked to the concessionary services.

17. The Danish legislation on passenger transport by bus and coach (Act No. 115 of 29 March 1978 with later amendments) and on goods transport by road (Act No. 851 of 21 December 1988 with later amendments) are based on the EEC directive No. 74/562/EEC on access to the market of passenger transport (respectively EEC directive No. 74/561/EEC on access to the market of goods transport by road – both amended by directive No. 89/438/EEC).

Denmark's current position under the Code of Liberalisation of Capital Movements and the National Treatment Instrument

Introduction

As a signatory to the OECD Code of Liberalisation of Capital Movements (the Code) and the National Treatment Instrument (NTI), Denmark has undertaken a number of obligations in the foreign direct investment field. The present annex highlights the main provisions of these instruments as well as Denmark's position under them.

The OECD commitments

The Code and the NTI are the two main instruments for co-operation among OECD member countries in the field of foreign direct investment.

The Code, which has the legal status of OECD Council Decisions and is binding on all Member countries, covers the main aspects of the right of establishment for non-resident enterprises and requires OECD members to progressively liberalise their investment regimes on a non-discriminatory basis and treat resident and non-resident investors alike.

The NTI is a "policy commitment" by Member countries to accord to established foreign-controlled enterprises treatment no less favourable than that accorded to domestic enterprises in like situations. While the NTI is a non-binding agreement among OECD Member countries, all measures constituting exceptions to this principle and any other measures which have a hearing on it must be reported to the OECD.

Member countries need not, however, liberalise all their restrictions upon adherence to the above instruments. Rather, the goal of full liberalisation is to be achieved progressively over time. Accordingly, members unable to fully liberalise are permitted to maintain "reservations" to the Code of Capital Movements and "exceptions" to the NTI for outstanding foreign investment restrictions. These limitations to the liberalisation obligations may be lodged at the time a member adheres to the Codes, whenever specific obligations begin to apply to a member, or whenever new obligations are added to the instruments.

The investment obligations of the Code and the NTI are, in fact, complementary, both dealing with the laws, policies and practices of Member countries in the field of direct investment. However, the Code addresses the subject from the point of view of non-resident investors in an OECD host country, while the NTI is concerned with the rights of established foreign-controlled enterprises. Limitations on non-resident (as opposed to resident) investors affecting the enterprises' operations and other requirements set at the time of entry or establishment are covered by the Code. The investment operations of foreign-controlled enterprises after entry, including new investment, are covered by the National Treatment Instrument.

Measures pertaining to subsidiaries fall under the purview of the Code or the NTI, depending on whether they set conditions on entry/establishment or concern the activities of foreign-controlled enterprises already established. As to branches, the 1991 *Review of the OECD Declaration and Decisions on International Investment and Multinational Enterprises* introduced a distinction between ''direct'' branches of non-resident enterprises and ''indirect'' branches, that is branches of already established foreign-controlled enterprises. The latter are subject to all the five categories of measures covered by the NTI (investment by established enterprises, government procurement, official aids and subsidies, access to local financing and tax obligations). The investment activities of ''direct'' branches of non-resident enterprises, which concern the category of measures covered by the NTI, fall however, exclusively under the purview of the Code.

The Committee on Capital Movements and Invisible Transactions and the Committee on International Investment and Multinational Enterprises together conduct country examinations of Member country measures covered by these OECD commitments. These examinations involve a face to face discussion between representatives of the two Committees and experts from the country being examined. The discussion is based on submission by the Member concerned and a document prepared by the Secretariat. The objective is to clarify the nature and purpose of remaining restrictions and to identify possible areas for further liberalisation. The examinations usually conclude with modifications to the Member country's position and recommendations by the OECD Council to the Member's authorities concerning the future direction of the country's foreign direct investment policies.

Denmark's position under the Code and the National Treatment Instrument

a) Denmark's reservations on foreign direct investment under the Code of Liberalisation of Capital Movements

1. "*List A,   Direct investment:

    I/A

    – In the country concerned by non-residents.

       Remark: The reservation applies only to:

       i) *Ownership of Danish flag vessels by non-EC residents except through an enterprise incorporated in Denmark;*

       ii) *Ownership by non-EC residents of one-third or more of a business engaged in commercial fishing;*

       iii) *Ownership of an air transport license, which is reserved to EC residents."*

2. Denmark's position under Annex E to the Code of Liberalisation of Capital Movements:

    "Establishment of insurance companies originating in non-EC Member countries may be subject to a reciprocity requirement."

b) Measures reported as exceptions to the National Treatment Instrument

A. Exceptions at national level

I. Investment by established foreign-controlled enterprises

Air transport

Cabotage reserved to national carriers.

Air transport

Licence to operate an airline is granted only to companies majority-owned by Danish nationals.

Authority: Administrative practice.

Air transport

An aircraft may not be registered in Denmark unless it is predominantly owned by Danish nationals or by companies or other entities controlled by Danish nationals.

Authority: Law 408, September 1985, Ministry of Transportation.

II. Official aids and subsidies

None.

III. Tax obligations

None.

IV. Government purchasing

None.

V. Access to local finance

None.

B. Exceptions by territorial subdivisions

None.

C. Transparency measures at the level of national government

I. Measures based on public order and essential security considerations

a) Investment by established foreign controlled enterprises

Defence

Production of defence material reserved to domestic companies with at least 60 per cent Danish ownership. Foreign capital may hold only 20 per cent of the voting rights.

Authority: Law 400, 13 June 1990.

b)   Corporate organisation
None.

c)   Government purchasing
None.

d)   Official aids and subsidies
None.

II.   Other measures reported for transparency

None.

D.   Measures reported for transparency at the level of territorial subdivisions

None.

The Structure of the Danish Business Sector, 1992

Share of total business sector

	Employment	GDP[1]	Exports[2]
Manufacturing	31.2	25.6	77.2
of which:			
Food and beverages	5.4	5.2	7.6
Wood and paper	5.4	4.3	2.7
Chemicals	3.1	3.8	11.1
Machines and equipment	12.9	8.9	32.2
Construction	9.9	7.6	..
Tradeable services	57.1	65.8	22.8
of which:			
Retail and wholesale	17.4	17.6	..
Transport	8.7	9.6	..
Financial services	6.4	3.9	..
Business services	8.8	9.5	..
Household services[3]	5.5	4.2	..
Home services[4]	1.8	1.0	..
Memorandum items:			
Business sector share of total economy[5]			
Denmark	64.2	73.0	..
OECD[6]	73.5	81.2	..
Public sector as a share of total economy[5]			
Denmark	30.4	21.5	..
OECD[6]	18.7	13.4	..
Agriculture and fishing as a share of total economy[5]			
Denmark	5.6	3.9	..
OECD[6]	5.4	2.7	..

1. At factor cost.
2. Not including service exports from the construction sector.
3. Including auto repairs.
4. Household employment and charitable institutions.
5. 1990.
6. Largest eleven OECD economies.
Source: OECD, *National Accounts of OECD Countries.*

Annex 3

Statistics on Denmark's foreign direct investment

Table 1. **Types of direct investment flows, Denmark**

	Greenfield (%)	Mergers and acquisitions (%)	Other* (%)	Total	
				%	DKr million
1988					
Inward	2	43	55	100	5 762
Outward	12	33	55	100	6 022
1989					
Inward	9	41	50	100	13 581
Outward	16	50	34	100	17 323
1990					
Inward	5	37	58	100	11 692
Outward	12	53	35	100	12 014
1991					
Inward	2	14	84	100	11 097
Outward	17	40	43	100	15 391
1992					
Inward	7	33	60	100	6 556
Outward	10	33	57	100	11 740
1993					
Inward	9	32	59	100	11 629
Outward	13	37	50	100	10 811

* Do not comprise retained earnings and inter-company loans.
Source: Danmarks Nationalbank, Statistical Office, March 1994.

Table 2. **Direct investment position at end 1991 by country**

DKr million

	Foreign direct investment in Denmark	% of total	Danish direct investment abroad	% of total
OECD AREA	86	98.6	80	89.0
Europe	75	86.2	68	75.4
EEC	39	44.7	51	56.8
Belgium-Luxembourg	3	3.9	–	–
France	6	7.3	5	5.4
Germany	6	6.4	7	7.9
Ireland	1	0.6	2	2.1
Italy	1	0.6	1	0.8
Netherlands	11	12.2	5	5.0
United Kingdom	12	13.7	24	26.0
Other Europe	36	41.6	17	18.6
Nordic countries	32	36.5	12	12.7
Switzerland	4	4.8	5	5.6
North America	10	11.9	10	10.7
Canada	–	–	3	2.9
USA	10	11.8	7	7.9
Other OECD area	1	0.6	3	2.9
Japan	1	0.6	1	1.6
NON OECD AREA	1	1.4	10	11.0
Africa	–	–	1	1.0
Central and Eastern Europe	–	–	1	1.3
Latin America-Carribean	1	0.8	3	3.6
South and East Asia	1	0.6	4	4.9
DAEs	–	–	3	3.8
Other Asia	1	0.6	1	1.1
Other countries	–	–	–	–
TOTAL	87	100.0	90	100.0

Source: Danmarks Nationalbank.

Table 3. **Direct investment position at end 1991 by industry**[1]

DKr million

	Foreign direct investment in Denmark	% of total	Danish direct investment abroad	% of total
PRIMARY	6	6.8	2	1.8
SECONDARY	15	17.3	21	22.9
Food, beverages and tobacco	4	4.1	5	5.3
Chemical products	4	4.8	5	5.2
Mechanical equipment	4	4.5	4	4.2
Other manufacturing	3	3.9	8	8.2
TERTIARY	65	74.6	66	72.4
Construction	1	1.4	4	4.5
Wholesale and retail trade	27	31.2	14	15.1
Transport and storage[2]	8	8.8	10	10.8
Finance, insurance and business services	19	21.9	16	17.3
Other services	10	11.3	23	24.8
UNALLOCATED	1	1.4	3	3.0
TOTAL	87	100.0	91	100.0

1. The distribution by sector concerns the company in which investment is made.
2. Including Communication.
Source: Danmarks Nationalbank.

Annex 4

Statistics on direct investment flows in OECD countries

Table 1. Foreign direct investment in OECD countries: inflows 1971-1992[1]

US$ million

	Cumulative flows		Flows of foreign direct investment											
	1971-1980	1981-1990	1981	1982	1983	1984	1985	1986	1987	1988	1989	1990	1991	1992
Australia	11 295	39 965	2 349	2 286	2 994	428	2 099	3 457	3 872	7 892	7 718	6 870	4 763	4 947
Austria	1 455	3 274	318	207	219	116	169	181	402	437	578	647	359	940
Belgium-Luxembourg[2]	9 215	28 182	1 352	1 390	1 271	360	957	631	2 338	4 990	6 731	8 162	8 919	10 791
Canada[2]	5 534	11 448	-3 670	-831	243	1 313	-2 050	990	3 469	3 614	1 773	6 597	6 544	4 963
Denmark	1 561	3 388	100	136	64	9	109	161	88	504	1 084	1 133	1 530	1 015
Finland	376	2 838	99	-4	84	138	110	340	265	530	489	787	-247	396
France[2]	16 908	43 194	2 426	1 563	1 631	2 198	2 210	2 749	4 621	7 204	9 552	9 040	11 073	15 894
Germany	13 969	18 029	341	819	1 775	553	587	1 190	1 901	1 203	7 131	2 529	4 263	2 422
Greece	::	6 145	520	436	439	485	447	471	683	907	752	1 005	1 135	1 144
Iceland[2]	::	12	::	::	::	14	23	8	2	-14	-27	6	35	17
Ireland	1 659	1 212	204	241	168	119	159	-43	89	91	85	99	97	102
Italy[2]	5 698	24 888	1 153	605	1 200	1 329	1 071	-21	4 144	6 882	2 181	6 344	2 481	3 161
Japan[2]	1 424	3 281	189	439	416	-10	642	226	1 165	-485	-1 054	1 753	1 368	2 728
Mexico	::	24 178	2 835	1 900	2 192	1 542	1984	2 401	2 635	2 880	3 176	2 633	4 762	4 393
Netherlands	10 822	27 850	1 520	965	757	587	641	1 861	2 307	4 077	6 370	8 765	4 934	5 883
New Zealand	2 598	3 945	177	275	243	119	227	390	238	156	434	1 686	1 695	1 089
Norway	3 074	4 831	686	424	336	-210	-412	1 023	184	285	1 511	1 004	-291	720
Portugal[3]	535	6 256	177	145	150	170	218	166	367	692	1 577	2 594	3 168	2 994
Spain[2]	7 060	46 000	1 714	1 801	1 647	1 773	1 945	3 442	4 548	7 016	8 433	13 681	10 423	8 115
Sweden	897	8 676	182	361	223	290	396	1 079	646	1 661	1 809	2 029	6 315	241
Switzerland	::	12 432	::	::	286	520	1 050	1 778	2 044	42	2 254	4 458	2 613	465
Turkey[4]	228	2 340	95	55	46	113	99	125	106	354	663	684	810	844
United Kingdom	40 503	130 477	5 891	5 286	5 132	-241	5 780	8 557	15 450	21 356	30 369	32 897	15 934	18 165
United States	56 276	368 309	25 195	13 810	11 518	25 567	20 490	36 145	59 581	58 571	69 010	48 422	25 446	3 388
TOTAL	188 249	821 150	43 853	32 309	33 034	37 282	38 951	67 307	111 145	130 845	162 599	163 825	118 129	94 817

1. Data updated in June 1994. Including data for Mexico who became a Member of OECD on 18 May 1994.
2. Reinvested earnings are not included in national statistics.
3. Figures for Portugal are only available from 1975 onward.
4. Cumulated inflows since 1954.
Source: OECD/DAF – Based on official national statistics from the balance of payments converted in US$ at daily average exchange rate.

Table 2.   Foreign direct investment in OECD countries: inflows 1981-1992[1]

As a percentage of GDP

	1981	1982	1983	1984	1985	1986	1987	1988	1989	1990	1991	1992
Australia	1.4	1.4	1.8	0.2	1.3	2.1	2.0	3.2	2.7	2.3	1.6	1.7
Austria	0.5	0.3	0.3	0.2	0.3	0.2	0.3	0.3	0.5	0.4	0.2	0.5
Belgium-Luxembourg[2]	1.3	1.6	1.5	0.4	1.1	0.5	1.6	3.2	4.2	4.1	4.3	4.7
Canada[2]	-1.2	-0.3	0.1	0.4	-0.6	0.3	0.8	0.7	0.3	1.2	1.1	0.9
Denmark	0.2	0.2	0.1	0.0	0.2	0.2	0.1	0.5	1.0	0.9	1.2	0.7
Finland	0.2	0.0	0.2	0.3	0.2	0.5	0.3	0.5	0.4	0.6	1.2	0.7
France[2]	0.4	0.3	0.3	0.4	0.4	0.4	0.5	0.7	1.0	0.8	-0.2	0.4
Germany	0.1	0.1	0.3	0.1	0.1	0.1	0.2	0.1	0.6	0.2	0.9	1.2
Greece	1.4	1.1	1.3	1.4	1.3	1.2	1.5	1.7	1.4	1.5	0.3	0.1
Iceland[2]	0.0	0.0	0.0	0.5	0.8	0.2	0.0	-0.2	-0.5	0.1	1.6	1.5
Ireland	1.1	1.3	0.9	0.7	0.8	-0.2	0.3	0.3	0.2	0.2	0.5	0.3
Italy[2]	0.3	0.2	0.3	0.3	0.3	-0.0	0.5	0.8	0.3	0.6	0.2	0.2
Japan[2]	0.0	0.0	0.0	-0.0	0.0	0.0	0.0	-0.0	-0.0	0.1	0.2	0.3
Mexico	1.2	1.9	1.8	1.0	1.9	2.8	3.0	1.7	1.7	1.1	1.7	1.3
Netherlands	1.1	0.7	0.6	0.5	0.5	1.0	1.1	1.8	2.8	3.1	1.7	1.8
New Zealand	0.7	1.2	1.0	0.5	1.0	1.4	0.7	0.4	1.0	3.9	4.0	2.6
Norway	1.2	0.8	0.6	-0.4	-0.7	1.5	0.2	0.3	1.7	1.0	-0.3	0.6
Portugal	0.7	0.6	0.7	0.9	1.1	0.6	1.0	1.7	3.5	4.3	4.6	3.6
Spain[2]	0.9	1.0	1.0	1.1	1.2	1.5	1.6	2.0	2.2	2.8	2.0	1.4
Sweden	0.2	0.4	0.2	0.3	0.4	0.8	0.4	0.9	0.9	0.9	2.6	0.1
Switzerland	0.0	0.0	0.3	0.6	1.1	1.3	1.2	0.0	1.3	2.0	1.1	0.2
Turkey	0.2	0.1	0.1	0.2	0.2	0.2	0.2	0.5	0.8	0.6	0.7	0.8
United Kingdom	1.2	1.1	1.1	-0.1	1.3	1.5	2.2	2.6	3.6	3.4	1.6	1.7
United States	0.8	0.4	0.3	0.7	0.5	0.9	1.3	1.2	1.3	0.9	0.5	0.1

1.   Data updated in June 1994. Including data for Mexico who became a Member of OECD on 18 May 1994.
2.   Reinvested earnings are not included in national statistics.
Source: OECD/DAF - Based on official national statistics from the balance of payments.

Table 3. Direct investment abroad from OECD countries: outflows 1971-1992 [1]

US$ million

	Cumulative flows		Flows of foreign direct investment											
	1971-1980	1981-1990	1981	1982	1983	1984	1985	1986	1987	1988	1989	1990	1991	1992
Australia	2 510	23 102	734	693	518	1 402	1 887	3 419	5 096	5 074	3 267	1 012	2 026	-197
Austria	578	4 132	206	142	190	68	74	313	312	309	855	1 663	1 288	1 871
Belgium-Luxembourg [2]	3 213	21 454	30	-77	358	282	231	1 627	2 680	3 609	6 114	6 600	6 062	10 891
Canada [2]	11 335	39 571	5 756	709	2 758	2 277	2 855	4 066	7 069	5 278	4 603	4 200	5 409	3 723
Denmark	1 063	6 292	141	77	159	93	303	646	618	719	2 027	1 509	1 851	2 225
Finland	605	12 132	129	85	143	493	352	810	1 141	2 608	3 108	3 263	1 049	406
France [2]	13 940	85 618	4 615	3 063	1 841	2 126	2 226	5 230	8 704	12 756	18 137	26 920	20 501	19 097
Germany	24 846	86 573	3 860	2 481	3 170	4 389	4 804	9 616	9 105	11 431	14 549	23 168	22 879	17 715
Iceland [2]	..	27	..	..	..	..	..	2	7	1	8	9	10	27
Italy [2]	3 597	28 707	1 425	1 025	2 133	2 012	1 820	2 652	2 339	5 554	2 135	7 612	7 326	5 956
Japan [2]	18 052	185 826	4 894	4 540	3 612	5 965	6 452	14 480	19 519	34 210	44 130	48 024	30 726	17 222
Netherlands	27 829	52 952	3 629	2 610	2 098	2 530	2 829	3 147	7 087	4 073	11 521	13 428	11 997	12 669
New Zealand	375	4 563	103	87	404	31	174	87	562	615	135	2 365	1 472	391
Norway	1 079	8 995	185	317	360	612	1 228	1 605	890	968	1 352	1 478	1 840	434
Portugal [3]	21	374	16	9	17	8	15	-2	-16	77	85	165	474	719
Spain [2]	1 274	8 196	272	505	245	249	252	377	754	1 227	1 470	2 845	3 574	1 273
Sweden	4 597	47 725	854	1 237	1 459	1 506	1 783	3 947	4 789	7 468	10 189	14 493	7 026	1 219
Switzerland	..	31 858	..	..	492	1 139	4 572	1 461	1 274	8 696	7 852	6 372	6 543	4 899
Turkey [4]	..	-7	..	..	..	..	..	..	9	–	–	-16	27	65
United Kingdom	55 112	185 674	12 065	7 145	8 211	8 039	10 818	17 077	31 308	37 110	35 172	18 729	15 597	16 571
United States	134 354	171 626	9 623	1 078	6 686	11 649	12 724	17 706	28 980	17 871	37 604	27 705	32 098	37 122
TOTAL	302 306	1 005 390	48 537	25 726	34 854	44 870	55 399	88 266	132 227	159 654	204 313	211 544	179 775	154 298

1. Data updated in June 1994. No data available on outflows for Mexico.
2. Reinvested earnings are not included in national statistics.
3. Figures for Portugal are only available from 1975 onward.
4. Includes cumulative investment since 1954.

Source: OECD/DAF - Based on official national statistics from the balance of payments converted in US$ at daily average exchange rate.

Table 4. Direct investment abroad from OECD countries: outflows 1981-1992[1]

As a percentage of GDP

	1981	1982	1983	1984	1985	1986	1987	1988	1989	1990	1991	1992
Australia	0.4	0.4	0.3	0.8	1.2	2.0	2.6	2.0	1.2	0.3	0.7	-0.1
Austria	0.3	0.2	0.3	0.1	0.1	0.3	0.3	0.2	0.7	1.0	0.8	1.0
Belgium-Luxembourg[2]	0.0	-0.1	0.4	0.4	0.3	1.4	1.8	2.3	3.8	3.3	2.9	4.7
Canada[2]	2.0	0.2	0.8	0.7	0.8	1.1	1.7	1.1	0.8	0.7	0.9	0.7
Denmark	0.2	0.1	0.3	0.2	0.5	0.8	0.6	0.7	1.9	1.2	1.4	1.6
Finland	0.3	0.2	0.3	1.0	0.7	1.2	1.3	2.5	2.7	2.4	0.9	0.4
France[2]	0.8	0.6	0.4	0.4	0.4	0.7	1.0	1.3	1.9	2.3	1.7	1.4
Germany	0.6	0.4	0.5	0.7	0.8	1.1	0.8	1.0	1.2	1.5	1.4	1.0
Iceland[2]	0.0	0.0	0.0	0.0	0.0	0.1	0.1	0.0	0.1	0.1	0.2	0.4
Italy[2]	0.3	0.3	0.5	0.5	0.5	0.4	0.3	0.7	0.2	0.7	0.6	0.5
Japan[2]	0.4	0.4	0.3	0.5	0.5	0.7	0.8	1.2	1.5	1.6	0.9	0.5
Netherlands	2.5	1.9	1.5	2.0	2.2	1.8	3.3	1.8	5.0	4.7	4.1	4.0
New Zealand	0.4	0.4	1.7	0.1	0.8	0.3	1.5	1.4	0.3	5.4	3.5	0.9
Norway	0.3	0.6	0.7	1.1	2.1	2.3	1.1	1.1	1.5	1.4	1.7	0.4
Portugal	0.1	0.0	0.1	0.0	0.1	0.0	-0.0	0.2	0.2	0.3	0.7	0.9
Spain[2]	0.1	0.3	0.2	0.2	0.2	0.2	0.3	0.4	0.4	0.6	0.7	0.2
Sweden	0.7	1.2	1.6	1.6	1.8	3.0	3.0	4.1	5.3	6.3	2.9	0.5
Switzerland	0.0	0.0	0.5	1.3	4.9	1.1	0.7	4.7	4.4	2.8	2.8	2.0
Turkey	0.0	0.0	0.0	0.0	0.0	0.0	0.0	0.0	0.0	0.0	0.0	0.1
United Kingdom	2.4	1.5	1.8	1.9	2.4	3.0	4.5	4.4	4.2	1.9	1.5	1.6
United States	0.3	0.0	0.2	0.3	0.3	0.4	0.6	0.4	0.7	0.5	0.6	0.6

1. Data updated in June 1994. No data available on outflows for Mexico.
2. Reinvested earnings are not included in national statistics.
Source: OECD/DAF - Based on official national statistics from the balance of payments.

MAIN SALES OUTLETS OF OECD PUBLICATIONS
PRINCIPAUX POINTS DE VENTE DES PUBLICATIONS DE L'OCDE

ARGENTINA – ARGENTINE
Carlos Hirsch S.R.L.
Galería Güemes, Florida 165, 4° Piso
1333 Buenos Aires   Tel. (1) 331.1787 y 331.2391
                    Telefax: (1) 331.1787

AUSTRALIA – AUSTRALIE
D.A. Information Services
648 Whitehorse Road, P.O.B 163
Mitcham, Victoria 3132   Tel. (03) 873.4411
                            Telefax: (03) 873.5679

AUSTRIA – AUTRICHE
Gerold & Co.
Graben 31
Wien I   Tel. (0222) 533.50.14

BELGIUM – BELGIQUE
Jean De Lannoy
Avenue du Roi 202
B-1060 Bruxelles   Tel. (02) 538.51.69/538.08.41
                   Telefax: (02) 538.08.41

CANADA
Renouf Publishing Company Ltd.
1294 Algoma Road
Ottawa, ON K1B 3W8   Tel. (613) 741.4333
                         Telefax: (613) 741.5439
Stores:
61 Sparks Street
Ottawa, ON K1P 5R1   Tel. (613) 238.8985
211 Yonge Street
Toronto, ON M5B 1M4   Tel. (416) 363.3171
                         Telefax: (416)363.59.63
Les Éditions La Liberté Inc.
3020 Chemin Sainte-Foy
Sainte-Foy, PQ G1X 3V6   Tel. (418) 658.3763
                            Telefax: (418) 658.3763
Federal Publications Inc.
165 University Avenue, Suite 701
Toronto, ON M5H 3B8   Tel. (416) 860.1611
                         Telefax: (416) 860.1608
Les Publications Fédérales
1185 Université
Montréal, QC H3B 3A7   Tel. (514) 954.1633
                          Telefax : (514) 954.1635

CHINA – CHINE
China National Publications Import
Export Corporation (CNPIEC)
16 Gongti E. Road, Chaoyang District
P.O. Box 88 or 50
Beijing 100704 PR   Tel. (01) 506.6688
                         Telefax: (01) 506.3101

CZECH REPUBLIC – RÉPUBLIQUE TCHÈQUE
Artia Pegas Press Ltd.
Narodni Trida 25
POB 825
111 21 Praha 1   Tel. 26.65.68
                         Telefax: 26.20.81

DENMARK – DANEMARK
Munksgaard Book and Subscription Service
35, Nørre Søgade, P.O. Box 2148
DK-1016 København K   Tel. (33) 12.85.70
                         Telefax: (33) 12.93.87

EGYPT – ÉGYPTE
Middle East Observer
41 Sherif Street
Cairo   Tel. 392.6919
                         Telefax: 360-6804

FINLAND – FINLANDE
Akateeminen Kirjakauppa
Keskuskatu 1, P.O. Box 128
00100 Helsinki
Subscription Services/Agence d'abonnements :
P.O. Box 23
00371 Helsinki   Tel. (358 0) 12141
                         Telefax: (358 0) 121.4450

FRANCE
OECD/OCDE
Mail Orders/Commandes par correspondance:
2, rue André-Pascal
75775 Paris Cedex 16   Tel. (33-1) 45.24.82.00
                          Telefax: (33-1) 49.10.42.76
                          Telex: 640048 OCDE
Orders via Minitel, France only/
Commandes par Minitel, France exclusivement :
36 15 OCDE
OECD Bookshop/Librairie de l'OCDE :
33, rue Octave-Feuillet
75016 Paris   Tel. (33-1) 45.24.81.67
                                  (33-1) 45.24.81.81
Documentation Française
29, quai Voltaire
75007 Paris   Tel. 40.15.70.00
Gibert Jeune (Droit-Économie)
6, place Saint-Michel
75006 Paris   Tel. 43.25.91.19
Librairie du Commerce International
10, avenue d'Iéna
75016 Paris   Tel. 40.73.34.60
Librairie Dunod
Université Paris-Dauphine
Place du Maréchal de Lattre de Tassigny
75016 Paris   Tel. (1) 44.05.40.13
Librairie Lavoisier
11, rue Lavoisier
75008 Paris   Tel. 42.65.39.95
Librairie L.G.D.J. - Montchrestien
20, rue Soufflot
75005 Paris   Tel. 46.33.89.85
Librairie des Sciences Politiques
30, rue Saint-Guillaume
75007 Paris   Tel. 45.48.36.02
P.U.F.
49, boulevard Saint-Michel
75005 Paris   Tel. 43.25.83.40
Librairie de l'Université
12a, rue Nazareth
13100 Aix-en-Provence   Tel. (16) 42.26.18.08
Documentation Française
165, rue Garibaldi
69003 Lyon   Tel. (16) 78.63.32.23
Librairie Decitre
29, place Bellecour
69002 Lyon   Tel. (16) 72.40.54.54

GERMANY – ALLEMAGNE
OECD Publications and Information Centre
August-Bebel-Allee 6
D-53175 Bonn   Tel. (0228) 959.120
                         Telefax: (0228) 959.12.17

GREECE – GRÈCE
Librairie Kauffmann
Mavrokordatou 9
106 78 Athens   Tel. (01) 32.55.321
                         Telefax: (01) 36.33.967

HONG-KONG
Swindon Book Co. Ltd.
13–15 Lock Road
Kowloon, Hong Kong   Tel. 2376.2062
                         Telefax: 2376.0685

HUNGARY – HONGRIE
Euro Info Service
Margitsziget, Európa Ház
1138 Budapest   Tel. (1) 111.62.16
                         Telefax : (1) 111.60.61

ICELAND – ISLANDE
Mál Mog Menning
Laugavegi 18, Pósthólf 392
121 Reykjavik   Tel. 162.35.23

INDIA – INDE
Oxford Book and Stationery Co.
Scindia House
New Delhi 110001   Tel.(11) 331.5896/5308
                         Telefax: (11) 332.5993
17 Park Street
Calcutta 700016   Tel. 240832

INDONESIA – INDONÉSIE
Pdii-Lipi
P.O. Box 4298
Jakarta 12042   Tel. (21) 573.34.67
                         Telefax: (21) 573.34.67

IRELAND – IRLANDE
Government Supplies Agency
Publications Section
4/5 Harcourt Road
Dublin 2   Tel. 661.31.11
                         Telefax: 478.06.45

ISRAEL
Praedicta
5 Shatner Street
P.O. Box 34030
Jerusalem 91430   Tel. (2) 52.84.90/1/2
                         Telefax: (2) 52.84.93
R.O.Y.
P.O. Box 13056
Tel Aviv 61130   Tel. (3) 49.61.08
                         Telefax (3) 544.60.39

ITALY – ITALIE
Libreria Commissionaria Sansoni
Via Duca di Calabria 1/1
50125 Firenze   Tel. (055) 64.54.15
                         Telefax: (055) 64.12.57
Via Bartolini 29
20155 Milano   Tel. (02) 36.50.83
Editrice e Libreria Herder
Piazza Montecitorio 120
00186 Roma   Tel. 679.46.28
                         Telefax: 678.47.51
Libreria Hoepli
Via Hoepli 5
20121 Milano   Tel. (02) 86.54.46
                         Telefax: (02) 805.28.86
Libreria Scientifica
Dott. Lucio de Biasio 'Aeiou'
Via Coronelli, 6
20146 Milano   Tel. (02) 48.95.45.52
                         Telefax: (02) 48.95.45.48

JAPAN – JAPON
OECD Publications and Information Centre
Landic Akasaka Building
2-3-4 Akasaka, Minato-ku
Tokyo 107   Tel. (81.3) 3586.2016
                         Telefax: (81.3) 3584.7929

KOREA – CORÉE
Kyobo Book Centre Co. Ltd.
P.O. Box 1658, Kwang Hwa Moon
Seoul   Tel. 730.78.91
                         Telefax: 735.00.30

MALAYSIA – MALAISIE
University of Malaya Bookshop
University of Malaya
P.O. Box 1127, Jalan Pantai Baru
59700 Kuala Lumpur
Malaysia   Tel. 756.5000/756.5425
                         Telefax: 756.3246

MEXICO – MEXIQUE
Revistas y Periodicos Internacionales S.A. de C.V.
Florencia 57 - 1004
Mexico, D.F. 06600   Tel. 207.81.00
                         Telefax : 208.39.79

NETHERLANDS – PAYS-BAS
SDU Uitgeverij Plantijnstraat
Externe Fondsen
Postbus 20014
2500 EA's-Gravenhage   Tel. (070) 37.89.880
Voor bestellingen: Telefax: (070) 34.75.778

NEW ZEALAND
NOUVELLE-ZÉLANDE
Legislation Services
P.O. Box 12418
Thorndon, Wellington   Tel. (04) 496.5652
    Telefax: (04) 496.5698

NORWAY – NORVÈGE
Narvesen Info Center – NIC
Bertrand Narvesens vei 2
P.O. Box 6125 Etterstad
0602 Oslo 6   Tel. (022) 57.33.00
    Telefax: (022) 68.19.01

PAKISTAN
Mirza Book Agency
65 Shahrah Quaid-E-Azam
Lahore 54000   Tel. (42) 353.601
    Telefax: (42) 231.730

PHILIPPINE – PHILIPPINES
International Book Center
5th Floor, Filipinas Life Bldg.
Ayala Avenue
Metro Manila   Tel. 81.96.76
    Telex 23312 RHP PH

PORTUGAL
Livraria Portugal
Rua do Carmo 70-74
Apart. 2681
1200 Lisboa   Tel.: (01) 347.49.82/5
    Telefax: (01) 347.02.64

SINGAPORE – SINGAPOUR
Gower Asia Pacific Pte Ltd.
Golden Wheel Building
41, Kallang Pudding Road, No. 04-03
Singapore 1334   Tel. 741.5166
    Telefax: 742.9356

SPAIN – ESPAGNE
Mundi-Prensa Libros S.A.
Castelló 37, Apartado 1223
Madrid 28001   Tel. (91) 431.33.99
    Telefax: (91) 575.39.98

Libreria Internacional AEDOS
Consejo de Ciento 391
08009 – Barcelona   Tel. (93) 488.30.09
    Telefax: (93) 487.76.59

Llibreria de la Generalitat
Palau Moja
Rambla dels Estudis, 118
08002 – Barcelona
    (Subscripcions) Tel. (93) 318.80.12
    (Publicacions) Tel. (93) 302.67.23
    Telefax: (93) 412.18.54

SRI LANKA
Centre for Policy Research
c/o Colombo Agencies Ltd.
No. 300-304, Galle Road
Colombo 3   Tel. (1) 574240, 573551-2
    Telefax: (1) 575394, 510711

SWEDEN – SUÈDE
Fritzes Information Center
Box 16356
Regeringsgatan 12
106 47 Stockholm   Tel. (08) 690.90.90
    Telefax: (08) 20.50.21

Subscription Agency/Agence d'abonnements :
Wennergren-Williams Info AB
P.O. Box 1305
171 25 Solna   Tel. (08) 705.97.50
    Téléfax : (08) 27.00.71

SWITZERLAND – SUISSE
Maditec S.A. (Books and Periodicals - Livres
et périodiques)
Chemin des Palettes 4
Case postale 266
1020 Renens VD 1   Tel. (021) 635.08.65
    Telefax: (021) 635.07.80

Librairie Payot S.A.
4, place Pépinet
CP 3212
1002 Lausanne   Tel. (021) 341.33.47
    Telefax: (021) 341.33.45

Librairie Unilivres
6, rue de Candolle
1205 Genève   Tel. (022) 320.26.23
    Telefax: (022) 329.73.18

Subscription Agency/Agence d'abonnements :
Dynapresse Marketing S.A.
38 avenue Vibert
1227 Carouge   Tel.: (022) 308.07.89
    Telefax : (022) 308.07.99

See also – Voir aussi :
OECD Publications and Information Centre
August-Bebel-Allee 6
D-53175 Bonn (Germany)   Tel. (0228) 959.120
    Telefax: (0228) 959.12.17

TAIWAN – FORMOSE
Good Faith Worldwide Int'l. Co. Ltd.
9th Floor, No. 118, Sec. 2
Chung Hsiao E. Road
Taipei   Tel. (02) 391.7396/391.7397
    Telefax: (02) 394.9176

THAILAND – THAÏLANDE
Suksit Siam Co. Ltd.
113, 115 Fuang Nakhon Rd.
Opp. Wat Rajbopith
Bangkok 10200   Tel. (662) 225.9531/2
    Telefax: (662) 222.5188

TURKEY – TURQUIE
Kültür Yayinlari Is-Türk Ltd. Sti.
Atatürk Bulvari No. 191/Kat 13
Kavaklidere/Ankara   Tel. 428.11.40 Ext. 2458
Dolmabahce Cad. No. 29
Besiktas/Istanbul   Tel. 260.71.88
    Telex: 43482B

UNITED KINGDOM – ROYAUME-UNI
HMSO
Gen. enquiries   Tel. (071) 873 0011
Postal orders only:
P.O. Box 276, London SW8 5DT
Personal Callers HMSO Bookshop
49 High Holborn, London WC1V 6HB
    Telefax: (071) 873 8200
Branches at: Belfast, Birmingham, Bristol, Edin-
burgh, Manchester

UNITED STATES – ÉTATS-UNIS
OECD Publications and Information Centre
2001 L Street N.W., Suite 700
Washington, D.C. 20036-4910 Tel. (202) 785.6323
    Telefax: (202) 785.0350

VENEZUELA
Libreria del Este
Avda F. Miranda 52, Aptdo. 60337
Edificio Galipán
Caracas 106   Tel. 951.1705/951.2307/951.1297
    Telegram: Libreste Caracas

Subscription to OECD periodicals may also be
placed through main subscription agencies.

Les abonnements aux publications périodiques de
l'OCDE peuvent être souscrits auprès des
principales agences d'abonnement.

Orders and inquiries from countries where Distribu-
tors have not yet been appointed should be sent to:
OECD Publications Service, 2 rue André-Pascal,
75775 Paris Cedex 16, France.

Les commandes provenant de pays où l'OCDE n'a
pas encore désigné de distributeur peuvent être
adressées à : OCDE, Service des Publications,
2, rue André-Pascal, 75775 Paris Cedex 16, France.

1-1995

OECD PUBLICATIONS, 2 rue André-Pascal, 75775 PARIS CEDEX 16
PRINTED IN FRANCE
(21 94 53 1) ISBN 92-64-14428-5 - No. 47915 1995
ISSN 1021-5794